the
fuzzy
firm

ARJAN VAN DEN BORN

ISBN/EAN: 978-90-820123-1-6
Published by: Born To Grow (www.bornto.nl)

Design cover: Iris Borst (iborst@casema.nl)
Design content and illustrations: Henry Hennipman (www.movivo.nl)

INDEX

COLOPHON

The essence of our enterprises is changing by the advance of technology; why we produce, what we produce, and how we produce. Where the 20th century corporation focused on efficient production using labor and capital, the firm of 21st century will co-create and innovate using knowledge, networks, and entrepreneurship.

This book describes the imminent transformation of our firms from stable hierarchies to fluid networks. The project will become the dominant form of organization, large corporations will disintegrate in new network forms such as communities and crowds and new labor relations will emerge as innovation will become more important than organizational loyalty. During this transformation the boundary of the organization will become blurred; the fuzzy firm is born.

Based on a thorough top-down analysis of technology developments and the value creation process of knowledge firms this book is a must-read for anyone who is interested in the future of organization.

PREFACE

66 An ounce of practice is worth more than tons of preaching." Mohandas Gandhi

Sometimes I consider myself as part of a small minority of organizational scientists; i.e. those scientists who have dedicated themselves to conduct research about the information-based network economy. Looking at today's economy, one should think that the focus of scientific research would be primarily aimed towards new concepts such as networks, knowledge, and creativity and emerging businesses such as creative industries or professional services. But in fact most of our organizational research focuses on understanding large industrial corporations studying labor, capital, and the value of tangible products. Even our terminology and instruments are very much based on the outdated perceptions of the 19th and 20th centuries. No one wants to see the elephant in the room.

Although our world has radically changed in the last 25 years, most researchers and practitioners are simply denying it. As we speak, many economists around the world are still estimating Cobb-Douglas production functions. Economic agencies still rely on manufacturing sector information such as purchasing orders and inventories to determine the true state of 'the economy'. We naively or purposely forget that the core of the manufacturing sector (i.e. the people who are actually responsible for producing material products) is today considerably less than 10 percent of our total economy. Even in large manufacturing conglomerates, such as Sony or Apple, most employees are in reality service providers.

However, economists are not the only ones in severe denial. Organizational scientists prefer to study multi-national corporation with their emphasis on capital, hierarchy, processes, and products. Students of entrepreneurship prefer to study fast growing, ambitious, technology ventures, rather than the countless emerging solo entrepreneurs and the networks in which they operate. The truth is that organizational research is still directed by big and fast growing businesses which offer prestige, valuable networks, and great datasets to researchers. Unfortunately, this research does not necessarily add to our understanding of tomorrow's world.

The emergence of the new economy is not only ignored by academia. Many leaders in the business world still act as if they have large factories with ten thousands of employees working on the assembly line producing corporeal products. Their marketing heads and staff still discuss product characteristics and thus ignore the fact that, in services, value cannot be created. The concept of value in services is something that is cocreated. Managers and management consultants are perhaps the ones that are mostly in denial. Not only do they refute reality, but they reconstruct their own reality using outdated organizational models. Many of these models are useful when properly applied, such as Porter's Value Chain, but most of them are simply not applicable in the new information economy. The underlying assumptions of these models are almost never tested. As a result Frederick Taylor has still a firm grip on managers and management consultants. As a result they adopt techniques such as lean thinking and Six Sigma in the field of knowledge and service productivity. Although it is clear that some of these process methodologies are quite useful in manufacturing or near-manufacturing settings (e.g. back-office), they certainly aren't helpful in a world where networks and knowledge determine the creation of value. Here the key question is not how the work is done (process), but what work is done (content).

Even the media is not able to break through the culture of denial. One would perhaps expect journalists to ask the obvious questions, but generally journalists do not challenge the great hidden assumptions of the industrial production economy; that we can measure output, corporations need extensive control, and capital is instrumental to business success. Journalists are sometimes able to pinpoint the extreme mishaps which are the result of using unsuitable models of control to professional environments (e.g. inadequate performance metrics and benchmarks in health care and public management), but they are rarely willing or able to question and challenge the overall policies. Most journalists are raised with the same mental models as the directors, managers, and consultants. It is rare for a journalist to question the hidden assumptions of policy.

Finally, most politicians just seem to follow the mood of the general public, and, at least in Europe, they certainly do not lead the public debate. Liberal politicians just argue for more employee security and employee autonomy and conservative politicians merely dispute for more flexibility and control. The fact that we desperately need new organizational and societal models which combine security with flexibility and collaboration with autonomy is completely disregarded. It is not even on the agenda of the B players.

My interest in the network economy originated in my research into freelancing success; what does it take to be a successful freelancer and what does success exactly mean? One of the conclusions of my research is that networking and collaborating with others are the most important success factors, simultaneously with professional skills. Thus I became interested in collaboration arrangements of freelancers, which made me aware that freelancers are continuously collaborating and building new communities and other forms of cooperation. From my research into hiring practices of large firms I learned that firms are increasingly contracting out and, at the same time, are giving more autonomy to their employees. It seems that both firms and freelancers are rapidly converging into one model where autonomous professionals team up together on communities, networks, and platforms.

Of course, I am not the only researcher interested in the future of work. Many of the ideas that I present in this book have already been discussed. I have been influenced by remarkable authors such as Manuel Castells and Daniel Pink, and a number of other authors such as Lynda Gratton have already forecast a lot of the trends described in this book, as well as some other relevant trends that I have largely omitted here. Like most other people, I am standing on the shoulders of giants. The major part of this book is based on the research and writings of others as are evident by many citations. Nevertheless, I like to think that this book differs from all other books written on the future of work in two key aspects. First, I based my conclusions essentially on the ongoing changes in the production function. The production function of the information-based network economy is totally different than the one of the industrial economy, just as the production function of the industrial economy has largely replaced the production function of the rural economy. Just as the invention of the steam engine triggered new forms of work and thus ultimately set the wheels in motion that led to today's complex economy, the invention of the internet has set the wheels in motion for a new information economy. Hence, our arguments are not particularly based on observed trends, but rather on fundamental changes in the process of value generation due to technological progress. Second, the drawn conclusions of this book with respect to the future of work go far beyond the conclusions of most other books. Due to my work in researching freelancers, I no longer see the long-term employment contract as the crème de la crème of the working relation. I consider the long-term employment contract as just a way to craft working relationships. In some cases it is the best way, but not necessarily always.

Finally, this book is written to initiate an open dialogue. I would like to share my knowledge regarding mixing traditional employees with freelancers and other new forms of working relations such as crowds and communities. This study provides an overview of some of the latest insights of the organization literature and presents some practical examples. However, this book does not cover all the areas of the discussed subject, simply because it is still in developing stage. Therefore, I welcome all your suggestions, ideas and comments to improve our understanding of the gig economy and the fuzzy firm of the future.

CHAPTER 1:

INTRODUCTION

66 The reasonable man adapts himself to the world; the unreasonable one persists in trying to adapt the world to himself." George Bernard Shaw

The last annual meeting of the World Economic Forum (WEF) concluded that it is fair to say that capital is losing its status as the most important factor of production. The significance of capital is rapidly being replaced by creativity and knowledge. Klaus Schwab, the founder of the WEF concluded that history is repeating itself. Just as capital replaced labor during the process of industrialization, capital is now being superseded by human knowledge and creativity. In this respect, the CEO of Manpower Inc., Jeffrey Joerres, stated that the era of capitalism is being replaced by the era of talentism. The new challenge for organizations is to have the right business models and people practices in place which enable the conversion of networks and knowledge into value-added services and products.

The current transformation from capitalism to talentism shouldn't be a surprise to anyone studying the modern firm. Already in the 1990s Peter Drucker stated that the productivity of knowledge-workers would be the biggest challenge of the 21st century, especially in the more developed countries. He argued that this question is quite complex and that all potential solutions have far-reaching consequences. The challenge is to reinvent the core of the traditional firm since the purpose of the 21st century firm is not limited to satisfying the needs of shareholders. The primary principal of the new firm is satisfying both talents and clients. In short: the survival of the 21st century firm depends largely on its ability to deliver value to the encompassing network.

How it was

In the 1960s it was pretty clear who worked for a company and who did not. Once a year, the entire firm and its employees were photographed at the annual company getaway. Every person regardless of his or her position in the firm, whether an executive or a receptionist, a clerk or an assembly line worker would smile in the photo (Figure 1). Unfortunately, nowadays it is not so easy anymore to determine who should be invited for the annual company getaway. The boundaries of the firm aren't clear as they used to be. Many jobs are outsourced to external staff. Not only the supporting tasks such as catering, security, and maintenance, but even major activities are increasingly contracted out. Within the boundaries of the firm temps work at the call center, contractors work on IT projects, specialist firms advise on the marketing strategy, and the infrastructure is maintained in the cloud by a large service provider. The physical boundaries of the organization have become hazy.

Figure 1.   One big happy family?

Along with this transformation essential questions arise. What is the real core of the company? Who belongs to our company and who doesn't? The everyday practice shows that these difficult questions are not always easily answered. In the Netherlands and the UK, such dilemmas occur every year when the allocation of Christmas hampers is discussed; does the external staff receive a Christmas hamper as well?

What we miss

The enormous growth in the number of external staff has not been planned. Its increase has been largely organic. As the firms began to outsource an ever growing portion of the work, step by step, the role of external parties became bigger. It is therefore perhaps no surprise that even after almost twenty years of continuous growth of outsourcing a coherent strategic vision on the role and value added of external staff and on the importance of interaction between external staff and employees is still largely missing. Many important questions remain unanswered. What is the optimal percentage of external staff? Is this 10 or 90 percent, or is this a totally irrelevant question? For which roles, functions, or activities should a firm establish long-term relationships with employees? What is the role of external collaborators in the innovation strategy? Most firms are not able to answer such strategic questions.

Even if there is a coherent strategic vision on the role, the work, and the added value of external parties, it is often outdated and based on old-fashioned and incorrect assumptions. And in very dubious cases where there is a suitable, contemporary strategy, the execution of such a strategy is generally very poor, as we will see later. Valuable factors of production, professionals with scarce knowledge, are habitually treated as articles of trade. There is a strong focus on contractual relationships when dealing with the externals, namely on the cost cutting and efficiency, rather than effectiveness and innovation. Procurement is on the lead while the HR function is struggling with its role and added value.

How it will be

The timing of this book is rather awkward as the worst economic recession since the 1930s has not quite terminated yet. Most businesses are still in survival mode rather than growth mode. Businesses are certainly not ready to invest in human and social capital as these types of investments are often characterized by soft business cases and pretty doubtful procedures. Nevertheless, it seems that there are strong strategic reasons for companies to invest in people, knowledge, and networks as these factors would ultimately determine their chances of survival.

Lynda Gratton is fundamentally correct when she says that we are witnessing a shift in work of an almost unprecedented scale.[1] In the future firms will have to invest a much larger proportion of their income in human capital to ensure their survival. A much smaller amount of funds will remain for capital providers such as banks and shareholders. But the nature of the investment in human capital is different from what is commonly assumed.

---

1   Lynda Gratton (2011), The Shift – The Future of Work is already Here, Harper Collins, London.

Contrary to many popular management books, this study is not simply a campaign for more training and development. Merely spending more money to attract and retain talents, whoever they may be, doesn't seem to be a wise move.

The very essence of firms will need to adapt to accommodate the changing nature of work itself. If we really witness this shift in work, as many researchers argue, then firms will not be able to cope with that challenge by only altering some priorities and procedures. Consequently, the talented and networked individuals are the ones who possess the scarce means of production. They determine the future, not the firm. The firm has to change fundamentally to accommodate the new working relationship with the individual. This new working relationship will add market incentives, flexibility, and autonomy to the well-known traditional long term employer-employee relationship. These new working relationships are able to combine the advantages of the market (flexibility, autonomy, incentives) with the advantages of hierarchies (security, trust, knowledge sharing, decision making) and will be healthier both for firms and individuals.

This book dishes away the presumption that long-term relationships between employers and employees are necessarily better for building trusted bonds. People tend to confuse retention for loyalty and vice versa. In real life we see that many long-term relationships between employers and employees would only lead to mutual captivity rather than prolonged happiness. In such cases, worker and firm do not stimulate each other and the long-term contract only constrains both parties in their ambitions and happiness. Many organizations have turned into prisons for their staff. Freedom of thought, innovation, and experiment are hardly fostered. Similar to some marriages that are near-perfect and partners actually strengthen each other, while others fail miserably on every aspect. This study is meant to provide a more balanced picture of the long-term worker relationship as it is in real life and not the theoretical ones suggested by the academics. Further, it aims to shed light on the circumstances in which the long-term employer-employee relationship is ideal for value creation. Moreover, it demonstrates the circumstances where slackly coupled relationships lead to even higher levels of creativity and innovation. The optimal resourcing strategy and the most favorable relationship between a firm and an individual depend primarily on the actual production and value creation processes.

The changing pace has increased tremendously in the last decade making the current shift in work, already anticipated by Peter Drucker in the 1990s, a very relevant strategic issue for all organizations. Thus it may be the best time to launch this transformation from the industrial to the innovation era. You will agree after having read this book.

This book is divided into five parts. The first part (i.e. chapters 2, 3, 4 and 5) describe the main technological forces which drive the emergence of the information networked economy and describes the outline of this new economy, which this study refers to as 'gig economy'. The second part (i.e. chapters 6, 7, and 8) explains the impact of this new economic reality on the firm of the future; the fuzzy firm. An era where new forms of collaboration will be dominant. The third part portrays the main forms of capital of this fuzzy firm; networks (chapters 9), knowledge (chapters 10), and leadership (chapters 11). The fourth part (i.e. chapters 12 and 13) focuses on a particular and important aspect of fuzzy firms: the capability of the firm to find the right person for the right job. How should knowledge workers be managed? Finally, chapter 14 will look into the future and demonstrates that there will be striking similarities between tomorrow's firms and the ancient organizational forms back to the Middle Ages and even earlier. We will go back to the future.

PART I

THE FORCES SHAPING OUR NEW WORLD

CHAPTER 2:

THE RACE AGAINST THE MACHINE

❝ 'We may not be interested in chaos but chaos is interested in us.'
Robert Cooper

According to Professor Tyler Cowen our rate of innovation has slowed tremendously during the last decades.[2] He argues that the high point of human innovation was in the late 19th and early 20th centuries, which produced new chemicals (medicines such as antibiotics and fertilizers), electricity (light, refrigerator, radio, television), and the internal combustion engine (automobile, airplane). These strategic breakthrough innovations transformed the lives of our grandparents who saw the birth of air travel, the arrival of the first car, and the magic of radio and television. Our way of living today is not so different from those of our ancestors fifty years ago. We still watch television, drive an automobile, use planes and trains, and rely on drugs for pain relief. Perhaps it is reasonable to suggest that living norms haven't changed much since 1960 and that our recent rate of invention has not been very impressive given the historical standards.

However, there is at least one exception to the argument above which cannot be ignored: the advent of Information Technology (IT). Since the 1960s the

---

2   Tyler Cowen: The Great Stagnation: How America Ate All The Low-Hanging Fruit of Modern History, Got Sick, and Will (Eventually) Feel Better:

personal computer and its descendants, such as the game console, laptop, and tablet, have changed our world beyond imagination. The introduction of the internet with its enormous amounts of information and huge communication powers is probably the single most dramatic transformation of the past 25 years. It is easy to forget that it was only invented just over 20 years ago, in 1989, by the British scientist Tim Berners-Lee and that CERN, the European Physics Research Center, then the employer of Berners-Lee, published the first article on 'the new World Wide Web' only on August 6th, 1991. Another important breakthrough information technology has been the invention of mobile communication. Only 20 years ago (1991), the first GSM network was implemented in Finland (Radiolinja). On top of these revolutionary innovations, several smaller innovations have been gradually surfing. Although the arrival of web 2.0 is perhaps not a big step in terms of technology, the tremendous social and economic impact of social media cannot be denied. Even modest innovations and improvements may sometimes have drastic economic and social consequences. Just as the invention of standardized shipping containers in the early 1970s may not seem to have huge impact, it is this minor invention that has influenced the life of all human beings.

No doubt information technology will continue to play an important role in shaping our future. Social networking sites like Facebook, YouTube and Twitter are just over five years old and other computer technologies as cloud computing, big data, and localization based services are still in developing stage. We simply cannot ignore that the arrival of the computer has transformed the lives of many people on the globe rigorously with enormous social, economic, and political consequences. Perhaps it is appropriate to quote Manuel Castells here: '*Furthermore, we are only at the beginning of this technological revolution, as the Internet becomes a universal tool of interactive communication, as we shift from computer-centered technologies to network-diffused technologies, as we make progress in nanotechnology (and thus in the diffusion capacity of information devices), and, even more importantly, as we unleash the biology revolution, making possible for the first time, the design and manipulation of living organisms, including human parts*'. [3]

The impact of information technology on work
Even if professor Tyler Cowen is somewhat mistaken and IT is actually a considerably bigger invention than he believes, the question that still has to be answered is how these improvements in information technology will influence our daily life. More specifically, how do IT inventions affect work and the organization of work? This question may be a little too simplistic as there is no such thing as 'IT invention'. Every day millions of designers,

---

3   Manuel Castells (2000). Materials for an exploratory theory of the network society, British Journal of Sociology, 51, 5-24

programmers, scientists, and users come up with a range of new inventions to improve products and services, like a colony of ants building their nest. Nevertheless, many people have been making predicaments about the impact of IT on work. Perhaps the most famous one is Jeremy Rifkin.[4] In 1995, Rifkin predicted that unemployment would increase drastically and information technology would eliminate more than ten million jobs. He argued that only a small group of managers and white collar workers would reap the benefits of IT and that the middle and lower classes would pay a huge price due to substitution of their work by advances in IT. Luis Suarez-Villa goes even further than Rifkin.[5] In his book on techno capitalism he argues that because technology is getting more and more sophisticated, more production processes will be fully automated and human steps will thus be eliminated. Therefore, the cost of goods will in the future almost completely be determined by the price of its raw resources. In the eyes of Suarez-Villa services will turn into free public goods. Obviously the realization of this prediction would have tremendous consequences for all firms and individuals.

While the arguments of Rifkin and Suarez-Villa are intuitively appealing, as ATM machines replace tellers, and internet self-service solutions replace call center agents, it is not without criticism. Even though the advances in IT do lead to more efficient processes and less work, this does not mean that new technology is not capable of producing new jobs. This is simply not true. First of all, to create and maintain any self-service solution, you need designers, programmers, communication people, helpdesk, and many more workers. Second, the savings will be transferred to shareholders and clients who may develop new needs based on the new and emerging situation.

Figure 2.   The same standard tasks every day; something from the past?

4   Jeremy Rifkin (1995). The End of Work: The Decline of the Global Labor Force and the Dawn of the Post-Market Era.
5   Louis Suarze-Villa (2009). Technocapitalism: A Critical Perspective on Technological Innovation and Corporatism.

To establish a better understanding of the impact of IT on employment, we therefore need to look beyond the obvious. What kind of work will disappear and what kind will remain? Will we humans still perform standard, routine tasks in the future? Based on extensive research Frank Levy and Richard Murnane argue that all routine form of employment will slowly disappear through the rise of the computer.[6] All tasks that can be translated in simple 'If... then' statements will be automated. They reckon that only those tasks which require complex forms of human knowledge or communication will not be replaced by IT. These are typically tasks that are one-off, which are aimed at change or innovation, and involve tacit knowledge. Levy and Murnane argue that this process of substitution (of man by machine) will proceed very fast. According to their research, in the 1990s alone the proportion of routine work decreased with nearly twenty percent. And since the beginning of this century this substitution process has accelerated further by the enormous investments of companies in online and self-service solutions. Routine forms of work are eliminated at an even faster pace than ever. Compiling these numbers, the claim that in the last 20 years the amount of standard-work has halved in the western world seems correct, leading to an increasing share of unique work in organizations (Figure 3).

The doom and gloom prediction of Levy and Murnane may even be too positive about the uniqueness of humans. There are indeed lots of activities which, back in 2004 when they carried out their research, were seen as uniquely human and which are nowadays almost routinely performed by computers. For example the autonomous car, also known as robotic or driverless car, is now a near reality. In regulated situations, driverless cars can already drive ten thousands of miles through daily traffic without human interference. Many companies such as GM, Volkswagen, BMW, Volvo, and Google have begun testing driverless car systems. GM has stated that driverless cars could be on the road by 2018, Volvo reckons that these cars can be produced as early as 2020. But as recent as 2004, Levy and Murnane kept arguing that these activities could never be performed by computers. And if we go back further in time, history is full of examples of capabilities that we once believed to be uniquely human. For instance in the 1990s many people were still convinced that humans' ability to play chess would always surpass the ability of computers, just because of our human creativity. Their beliefs were shattered in 1997 when Deep Blue, IBM's chess computer, won a six-game match from Gary Kasparov.[7]

---

6   Frank Levy & Richard J. Murnane (2004). New Division of Labor: How Computers Are Creating the Next Job Market.
7   After losing, Kasparov believed that he saw profound intelligence and creativity in the machine's moves.

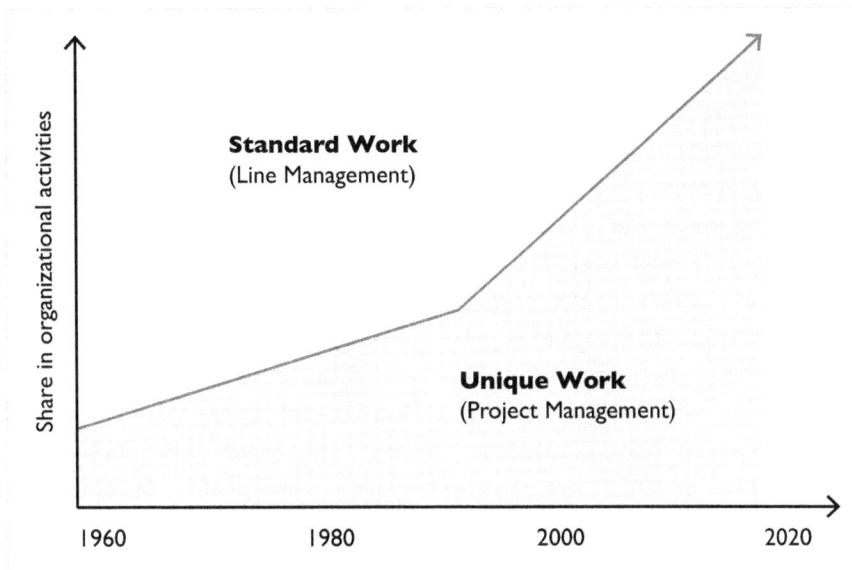

Figure 3.   The ever increasing importance of unique work

So computers are indeed steadily and swiftly replacing us humans, even for works that we considered to be typically human less than a decade ago. No single occupation seems to be safe from this advancement in technology. Although tasks which require complex forms of human knowledge and communication are more sheltered than standard routine tasks, it seems that even these tasks may eventually be replaced by IT. And if a certain task, how complex it may be, is performed frequently, the business case for automation is never far away. A great example of likely future automation of a typical 'human' task is the replacement of nurses by a robot.[8] Currently, the existing nursing robots merely assist nurses with lifting of heavy patients, but some universities are quite far with developing robots that are able to perform all standard duties of nurses such as bringing food, drinks, and medicine, as well as answering simple questions. Having robot-nurses in the future doesn't seem to be far away.

Erik Brynjolfsson and Andrew McAfee have been looking beyond the obvious and analyzed the empirical evidence on the relationship between IT and employees.[9] They conclude that there will be three sets of winners and losers within society.

1. **High skilled workers will replace low skilled workers.** Technologies like robotics, OCR, self-service internet have been replacing low skilled workers. At the same time other technologies like data visualization and data analytics have amplified the benefits of high-skilled workers.

---

8   http://blogs.vancouversun.com/2012/02/18/riba-the-robot-to-replace-nurses-and-caregivers-for-king-kong-like-patient-lifting-duties-in-japan/
9   Erik Brynjolfsson & Andrew McAfee (2011). The Race Against The Machine.

2. **Superstars are better off than everyone else.** This is due to the arrival of winner-takes-all markets. Brynjolfsson and McAfee propose that in every industry where digitization is employed only a little group of individuals or companies that reap the lion's share of the rewards. As we will see later in this study, this is a typical property of the new networked economy where there are enormous economies of scale for platforms and other network organizations.

3. **The share of labor is decreasing.** Susan Fleck, John Glaeser, and Shawn Sprague argue that capital is getting a bigger share of the pie as robots are replacing humans.[10] Their argument is in contrast to the prediction of many other investigators, such as Drucker and Suarez-Villa, who both argue that the share of capital will diminish as a result of the decreasing importance of capital as a production factor. Perhaps this contradiction can be explained by the fact that it is becoming increasingly difficult to distinguish between capital gains and labor income. Mitt Romney, for instance, recorded his rewards from his VC investments as capital gains, only to avoid taxes. And the gains of Marc Zuckerberg on the Facebook IPO will also be recorded as capital gains. Their winnings, in both cases based on their entrepreneurship, are recorded as capital gains. One could argue that these takings should not be considered to be capital income. Nor should it be counted as labor income like wages and bonuses of CEO's and professional athletes. Instead such earnings should ideally be regarded as entrepreneurial income.

The trend towards standardization

One of the most important trends in the last 25 years has been the standardization of systems and processes covering almost all kind of professions and capabilities. As early as the 1990s most organization still had their own organizational specific processes (i.e. this is the way we do things around here) and had developed customized IT applications to support these organizational specific processes. Nowadays these processes are performed by standardized IT systems which are increasingly procured 'from the shelf'. This implies that most business processes are nowadays pretty standard and certainly much less tailored to specific business circumstances than they were in the past. Today almost everyone uses MS Outlook (or a related product) for agenda management, the MS Office suite is used for text, spreadsheets, and presentations, SAP or another of the shelf ERP system is used for logistics and financial processes, Salesforce.com for CRM, Adobe Photoshop for editing pictures, and this list goes on and on. At the same time standard methodologies and processes are developed to guide the work of professionals (e.g. ITIL for IT maintenance, Prince2 for project management). The emergence of these standardized solutions and

---

10   Susan Fleck, John Glaeser, & Shawn Sprague (2011). (http://bls.gov/opub/mlr/2011/01/art3full.pdf)

homogenized processes has diminished the importance of organization-specific competencies (i.e. how do we work at company X?) in favor of industry-specific and professional competencies.[11] (Figure 4)

The declining relative importance of organization-specific competencies has many important consequences that are not always fully appreciated. One of the most obvious ones, as argued by Edward Lazear and Katryn Shaw, is that this decline in firm-specific skills will lead to a greater mobility of workers. For instance, in the earlier years of Silicon Valley computer programming skills were often firm specific (as for Oracle or Microsoft). As Silicon Valley developed, and markets thickened, many firms could now make use of what were once firm-specific skills and thus the mobility of workers rose.[12]

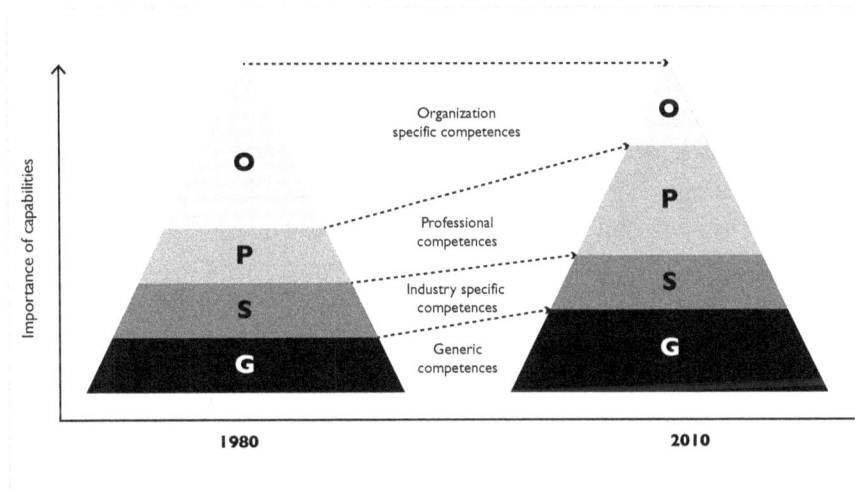

Figure 4.   *Professional knowledge dominates organizational knowledge*

The increased mobility of employees is often seen as a major risk for many companies, as high valued employees can leave the organization and use their skills for any competitor. But a high turnover of employees may actually be blessing in disguise as Anna Lee Saxenian shows in her famous book on Silicon Valley.[13] According to Anna Lee, Silicon Valley was able to establish itself as the world's premier region of technology just because of this frequent job-hopping as it fostered Silicon Valley's culture and tradition of openly sharing information. Anyway, the trend of diminishing organizational skills and, in parallel, expanding professional skills suggests that employees and employers are becoming less interdependent. The number of long-term symbioses between employees and employers will decline and, just as in

11   Paul Sullivan (2006). Empirical Evidence on Occupation and Industry Specic Human Capital, Bureau of Labor Statistics, MPRA Paper No. 863. http://mpra.ub.uni-muenchen.de/863/

12   Edward P. Lazear and Kathryn L. Shaw (2007). "Personnel Economics: The Economist's View of Human Resources." Journal of Economic Perspectives, 21, 91–114.

13   Anna Lee Saxenian (1994). Regional Advantage: Culture and Competition in Silicon Valley and Route 128.

Silicon Valley, employee turnover rates will increase. The British weekly The Economist described this as follows: *'The labor market rewards individual capital, being adaptable, knowing your industry, keeping your skills fresh and having a network of peers. The best way to build this is by changing jobs more frequently; a good job now must enhance your personal skill set which you can take somewhere else'.*[14] The increased importance of professional skills versus organizational skills will also lead to a rearrangement of industries and career ladders. The individual career will not be based along organizational ladders, but rather along professional ladders. This implies that individuals will want to work for organizations which help them develop their profession. Gradually more and more individuals will want to work for specialized professional firms and less for large broadly-based conglomerates.

The trend towards hyper specialization

Since the late 1970s one observes increasing levels of specialization of firms in almost all sectors. Large traditional players are ever more opposed by new entrants who focus on a specific value adding activity. This trend is visible in various sectors and industries such as consumer electronics, the computer business, and the car industry.[15] The synchronized occurrence of this trend is by no means an accident. In their theory on emerging industries Michael Jacobides and Stephan Billinger explain this ubiquitous drive towards specialization.[16] They start their argument by stating that potential benefits of cooperation always exist whenever organizations differ in their core capabilities. This is almost always the case. Specialization is however frustrated by high transaction costs. But when these transaction costs fall, for example because of the introduction of a new technological solution, the potential benefits of specialization will materialize in actual profits. They show that the advancement in IT technology would immediately lead to declining transaction costs which subsequently commence a perpetuating circle of ever-increasing specialization. Suppliers and purchasers develop and introduce new coordination mechanisms to facilitate collaboration between entities. This pattern of increased collaboration continues until a new industry composition emerges which divides the traditional generalist organizations into many different specialist firms with specific core competences (Figure 5).

Jacobides and Stephan Billinger's model describes the specialization of organizations within sectors, but could be applied to individuals as well as tumbling transaction costs also initiate the increased specialization of individuals. In a recent paper Tom Malone, Robert Laubacher, and Tammy

14 http://www.economist.com/blogs/freeexchange/2011/09/labour-markets
15 Baines Tim., Dan Whitney & C. Fine (1999). Manufacturing technology Sourcing practices in the USA. International Journal of Production Research, 37, 939-956.
16 Michael Jacobides & Stephan Billinger (2006). Designing the Boundaries of the Firm: From "Make, Buy, or Ally" to the Dynamic Benefits of Vertical Architecture. Organizational Science, 17, 249–261

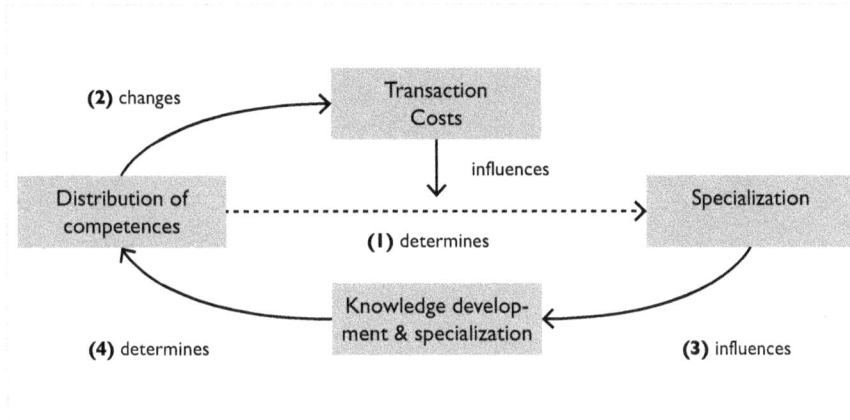

Figure 5. The perpetuating circle towards hyper specialization

Johns argue that the era of hyperspecialization is nigh. [17] Positions which are currently performed by a single person will in the future be carried out by many specialists working in distributed work concepts. Just as specialization of tasks led to more efficient processes in the industrial revolution, the current tasks of knowledge workers in the service sector of the economy will be increasingly taken over by global, complex networks of people with specialist tasks. This trend is triggered by two underlying influences. First, diminishing transaction costs would lead to increased specialization, following Jacobides and Billinger's model. Second, in the knowledge economy, the quality of the work performed is strongly correlated with the quality and experience of people who actually perform the work. Specialists are able to perform specialist work not only better, but also faster, and therefore cheaper.

Overview

1. In the western world we are rapidly eliminating and automating all routine tasks. Tasks that remain have an element of uniqueness.

2. With the introduction of automation professional knowledge becomes more important than organizational specific knowledge.

3. Due to diminishing transaction costs there is a tendency for hyperspecialization for both firms and individuals.

---

17   http://hbr.org/2011/07/the-big-idea-the-age-of-hyperspecialization/ar/1

CHAPTER 3:

CREATING VALUE IN THE INFORMATION ECONOMY

❝ A business absolutely devoted to service will have only one worry about profits. They will be embarrassingly large.❞ Henry Ford

As we stated earlier, our existing understanding of organizations and the economy is still very much based on studies of industrial production and manufacturing. Although our scientific and political fondness of industrial production with its economies of scale and great possibilities for export is understandable, it does not essentially help our understanding of the current economy. Perhaps the primary difference between the manufacturing industry and the service sector lies in the process of value creation. Adding value through intangible services is a totally different practice and much more difficult to grasp than adding value through the delivery of tangible products. Although the attention for services has been increasing, our understanding of the value creating process in services is still limited.

Service logic
First milestone demonstrating our increased awareness of the importance of services is the well-known SERVQUAL methodology. This methodology used to measure the quality of services was introduced by Zeithaml,

Parasuraman, and Berry in the early 1990s.[18] But the unique nature of services was only really put on the map as recent as 2004 when an influential article appeared written by marketing professors Stephen Vargo and Robert Lusch describing the true value creating principles of the service economy.[19] In this paper, Vargo and Lusch argue that our dominant logic, the way we think, is still largely based on the exchange of 'goods'. In order to understand the true meaning of the new economy, we need a revised logic as the value creation process is fundamentally different in services. Vargo and Lusch call this reasoning 'service-dominant logic' or 'SD-logic' and this logic is quite unusual in many aspects. Vargo and Lusch thus developed 10 foundational premises (FP) on which SD-logic is based and that differ from common thinking. This paper will not discuss all the 10 different premises of SD-logic, but will provide an overview of some of the most important premises. To begin with, value is always created in close cooperation with the customer as the consumer is an integral part of the production process (FP6; 'the consumer is always a cocreator of value'). Vargo and Lusch therefore would like to talk about prosumers instead of consumers. Second, FP6 implies that the role of the service provider is actually quite limited and cannot really deliver value (FP7; 'the company delivers no value, but value propositions'). Third, the relationship with the customer is essential in adding value (FP10; 'value is always uniquely and phenomenologically determined by the beneficiary ').

Although our comprehension of services in general and SD-logic in particular is rapidly developing and has a growing base of supporters, mainstream thinking is still very much rooted on old, outdated models originated on manufacturing industries. Even academic research in economics and business has primarily focused on large corporates producing tangible goods and the economies trading these goods.

Chains, networks, and shops

SD-logic teaches us that service provision rather than goods production is fundamental to economic exchange and value creation. But SD-logic can be quite conceptual sometimes and the theory does not give practitioners concrete and precise tips or techniques to create value. Fortunately, a more concrete model of value creation has been available for years; Michael Porter's famous value chain.[20] This great model of value creation decomposes a firm in a number of value generating activities. It enables a firm to assess it on these activities and allows it determine where it adds the most value to its customers. Regrettably, the value chain, as most models of

---

18 Valerie Zeithaml, A. Parasuraman & Leonard Berry (1990). "Delivering Quality Service; Balancing Customer Perceptions and Expectations," Free Press.
19 Stephen Vargo & Robert Lusch (2004) 'Evolving to a New Dominant Logic for Marketing', Journal of Marketing, 68, 1-17.
20 Michael Porter (1985). Competitive Advantage: Creating and Sustaining Superior Performance.

the 80s and 90s, is based on the production and trade of tangible goods. The value generating activities, from inbound logistics to marketing and sales, only apply to these traditional firms.

To understand how value is created in today's information-based network economy other configurations of value creation are warranted. The value chain is simply not appropriate. Charles Stabell and Øystein Fjeldstad have therefore developed two additional configurations of value creation: the value shop and the value network.[21] Although everyone can intuitively understand the meaning of value shops and value networks, the corresponding literature is not very renowned. For better comprehension of the creation method of value in the knowledge economy, Stabell's and Fjeldstad's value configurations are discussed below. The value chain will not be discussed here as Porter's framework is quite familiar to most scholars of organizational theory as well as the practitioners.

Configuration	Value Chain (Porter)	Value Shop	Value Network
Adds value by …	Transformation of input to output	Resolving customer issues	Connecting customers
Organization	Permanent	Temporary & permanent	Permanent
Value-added activities	1. Purchase 2. Operation 3. Distribution 4. Sales 5. Service	1. Define problem 2. Think of solutions 3. Choose solution 4. Perform solution 5. Evaluate solution	1. Promotion network 2. Contract management 3. Service provision 4. Take care of the infrastructure
Examples	Shell, Philips	McKinsey, Feature Film	ABN Amro, Linked In

Table 1.   Value chains, value networks, and value shops

Value shops are organizations of professionals on a certain knowledge domain. These professionals have developed a methodical approach, an intelligent framework, and specific knowledge to solve specific and complex questions. In today's economy the majority of organizations are in fact value shops. This is because the value shop configuration describes how professionals add value through the application of their knowledge and creativity. With the proliferation of complex problems and the corresponding mounting pressures to solve these byzantine knots, there is no surprise that an increasing proportion of all organizations are 'value shops'. In many cases, the entire industries are formed by value shops (e.g. industries such as health care or professional services), but value shops can also be found within large industrial conglomerates. For example, many

21   Charles Stabell & Øystein Fjeldstad (1998). Configuring Value for Competitive Advantage: On Chains, Shops, and Networks, Strategic Management Journal, 19, 413-437.

supporting departments in industrial conglomerates (IT, HRM, finance, and marketing) are basically value shops.

Typically value shops perform five different types of activities that add value to the customers. The first value added activity is 'defining the problem'. These include are all performed activities aimed to describe the problem properly and to formulate an approach to solve the problem at hand. The second value added activity is 'thinking of solutions' where possible solutions are formulated. The third value added activity is 'choosing the appropriate solution'. Fourth, 'realizing and implementing the solution' is the value added activity which is most obvious to clients and observers. Finally, value can be created in a value shop by 'evaluating the solution'. Here the results are evaluated (and measured) to determine whether the original problem still exists. It is clear that in such a context, where value is added by sensing and solving a difficult problem, the value-adding activities are entirely different from the value chain, where value is added by augmenting a product by adding ingredients. The value creation process of the value shop actually closely resembles William Deming's Plan-Do-Check-Act cycle.[22]

The most conventional way to enhance value for customers, which has been practiced for many centuries in any value configuration, is through specialization. In value chain configurations, organizations or individuals are specialized on a specific part of the value chain (e.g. procurement) or a specific product. This idea of specialization has been as old as the economy itself. Adam Smith, for instance, argues that economic growth is caused by the increasing division of labor where each worker becomes an expert in one isolated area.[23] A recognized and relatively recent example of value chain specialization in the UK is Kwik-Fit, a car servicing and repair company of Scottish origin. Their value proposition is based on low prices and quick services for a small segment where easy repairs and high volume are possible: tires, brakes, and exhaust pipes. With this proposition they reformed the UK car servicing market in the 1980s which caused serious problems for traditional automotive dealers who saw the rise of price competition on a market that used to be very lucrative. The car dealers were ultimately left with the more complicated and scarce repairs.

The phenomenon of ever increasing specialization can nowadays be observed in value shop industries. More and more organizations are specializing in a certain, very narrowly defined knowledge domain (e.g. HR Strategy) or in a specific activity of the value shop such as analyzing, selecting, or evaluating. An interesting example here is the U-test, a software testing company. What

22   William Deming (1986). Out of the Crisis. MIT Press.
23   Adam Smith (1776), The Wealth of Nations, W. Strahan and T. Cadell, London

makes the U-test unique is that they use new distributed work practices to test software. U-test is a combination of a value network (i.e. a community of specialists) and a value shop (i.e. expert professionals trained to evaluate the quality of software).

Case: U-test Crowd Source Testing: Outsourcing at its Best?

U-test is a crowdsourcing platform for software testing. With more than 45.000 testers in 180 countries, it is the largest online community of testers. With the exception of unit testing they perform all tests that ordinary Testing-As-A-Service (TAAS) parties supply such as functionality, usability, security, and load testing. Interestingly, testers get paid for every 'bug' they discover in the software. The benefits of crowdsourcing testing are:

- No 'bugs' = no costs
- Software is tested by hundreds of people at once
- Testers have different expertise
- Software can be tested in various languages by different kinds of people from a variety of nations and cultures
- Criticism of the software is delivered by external, independent professionals
- Quick feedback of test results

There are more crowdsourcing platforms of testers beside the U-test (e.g. Army, XBOSoft, and Mob4Hire). U-test is a platform aimed at evaluating software. There are other crowdsourcing initiatives that successfully evaluate developed products or services before they enter the market.

The **value network** is the third type of value configuration, next to value shops and value chains. Value networks enable parties to connect with each other, thereby creating value for all participants. Some value networks are already quite old (e.g. banks and insurance companies), but the information economy has led to an unprecedented growth in new network industries such as gaming, social media, and telecommunication. All these new value networks are basically modern forms of the old English 'business club' and have four different value-adding activities. 'Promoting the network' to potential customers is the first value-added activity. It is in this respect that one of the most crucial properties of these networks arise, the immense economies of scale in these types of companies. Size matters: most network sectors are dominated by a single player (e.g. Google, Apple, Facebook, and YouTube). These network economies of scale crop up because the more people join the network the larger the value of the network will be for other people. 'Managing the contract' is the second value-added activity in value networks. A clear overview of use, status, and benefits as well as costs of the network adds, in many cases, value to its members. As the third value adding activity is 'delivery of supplementary services', i.e. services besides contract management and network access. A bank can, for instance, offer a profitable savings account and various mortgage products to its network (i.e. customers) and Apple makes a large amount of money through music and apps offered on the i-Phone. 'Maintaining and optimizing the infrastructure' is the fourth and final value-added activity in a value network. Keeping the infrastructure up-to-date is absolutely important since an unavailable or slow network is fatal for the image of a value network.

The two additional value configurations of Charles Stabell and Øystein Fjeldstad describe the value creation process in today's information-based network economy much better than Michael Porters value chain. Their configurations demonstrate that value is not always created by enriching products, but that value in the information-based network economy is created by 1) linking participants in networks and 2) by solving complex questions. It should be noted that the three value creation configurations are not mutually exclusive. Many of today's businesses are in fact very intelligent combination of different value creating configurations which influence and, hopefully, strengthen each other. BMW is, for instance, in its core a manufacturing organization (i.e. a value chain). But at the same time BMW's design team adds value by designing new cars and BMW's engineers add value by inventing new engines, transmission, or suspension systems. These professionals create value through the value shop model. Finally, BMW is also harnessing the wisdom of crowds by creating communities, for instance, around its M-series of sportive cars. By creating such a community, BMW creates value through the value network. So BMW as a company is an intelligent combination of various value generating configurations and activities.

In 1950s, Robert Solow and Trevor Swan identified the major growth factors of the 19th and 20th centuries: the inputs of labor and capital.[24] Many other investigators and researchers such as Paul Romer, Robert Lucas, and Paul Krugman have showed since then that labor and capital are not sufficient factors anymore to explain production output. To understand the factors of production in the new information-based network economy, Charles Stabell and Øystein Fjeldstad, altogether with Stephen Vargo and Robert Lusch, point the way forward. In the future, value will still be created by labor and capital (as in the value chain), but knowledge (value shops), and networks (value networks) are becoming increasingly important. These upcoming factors of production will determine value creation in the 21st century. Hereby one should note that value is something which cannot be seen independent from the customer. In a service-economy, true value is always cocreated. This all implies that the production function has totally changed in the last decades. Labor and capital play still a part in the 21st century production

---

24 Robert Solow (1956). A Contribution to the Theory of Economic Growth. Quarterly Journal of Economics, 70, 65-94 & Trevor Swan (1956). Economic Growth and Capital Accumulation. Economic Record, 32, 334-361.

function, but the front seats are more and more reserved for networks, platforms, professional knowledge, innovation, and entrepreneurship.

Overview

1. The new economy is a service-oriented information economy. Value is cocreated not delivered.

2. New value configurations will dominate the economy. If the 20th century with its large manufacturing base was dominated by value chain, the service economy of the 21st century will be dominated by (combinations of) value shops and value networks.

3. Value networks aim to connect people. Because of their enormous economies of scale, an industry will have only a small number of value networks.

4. Value shops are aimed to solve specific problems. There are limited economies of scale. These value shops will largely operate on platforms created by networks.

5. New business models will emerge to combine characteristics of chains, shops, and networks.

CHAPTER 4:

THE GIG ECONOMY; EVERYONE WORKS IN PROJECTS

66 About 150 years ago, American workers began a profound shift from farms to factories. Now we find ourselves in the middle of an equally large transition: just as workers left the plow for the assembly line, they are now leaving the cubicle for the coffee shop." Sara Horowitz

Perhaps the most thought-provoking set of books of the last decades is *The Information Age* trilogy of Manuel Castells.[25] This fascinating trilogy studies human beings and their relationship towards production, consumption, and power in the information economy. Castells argues that our economy is very different from the old industrial economy for three distinct reasons:

1. It is an information economy. The capacities of processing information and generating newfound knowledge determine the productivity and competitiveness of humans, organizations, regions, and states.
2. It is a global economy. Core high-value economic activities can be performed everywhere around the globe and these tasks can be coordinated in parallel in real-time.
3. It is a networked economy. At the heart of the economy there is a new form of economic organization, the network enterprise. This is a new

---

25   Manuell Castells. The Rise of the Network Society (1996), The Power of Identity (1997), & End of Millennium (1998).

form of network enterprise rather than a network of firms. It is a network of individuals. Large organizations will be dismantled and internally de-centralized as networks. And small and medium enterprises will be connected in networks. These networks are created around specific projects, and these building blocks switch to other networks as soon as a project is completed.

The notion of a network economy is in itself hardly new. Various economic sectors have always been network economies. In the construction sector, for instance, contractors, subcontractors, and skilled employees all come together to create or recreate a building. These different professionals work temporarily together on the projects. The American feature film industry is another good example of a network economy. This sector is particularly interesting because of its transformation during the past 50 years from an industrially organized sector to a network economy. During this transition of Hollywood, from industrial sector to network sector, new markets materialized and new firms emerged which replaced the departments in the old hierarchies.[26] At the same time, existing players either vanished or adapted themselves and took on new roles. A brief outline of the transformation of the feature film industry can help us understand these forces of change.

Hollywood as an example

Up to 1960s there were five major movie studios in Hollywood: 20th Century Fox, Metro-Goldwyn-Mayer, Paramount, RKO, and Warner Bros. Directors, writers, actors, make-up artists, technicians, camera operators, and all other employees had little to say about their work or their career. They all worked for the studios and, for the most part, simply followed the orders. Even the big stars were tied to the studios by long-term contracts. The studios were in charge of their celebrities. They decided the type of roles they played, managed their publicity and public image. They even decided how (and with whom) they should live.

The feature film industry was so powerful because the five major movie studios controlled the whole production process, from production to distribution. The studios could decide which film played in which cinema. The primary focus of the studios was the efficient production of films by maximizing the utilization rate of their employees. The planners of the feature film companies determined which films were produced and which employees were deployed for which film. This system of production led to a massive profitable industry with limited risks, but also to a dormant

---

26   Douglas Gomery (2008). The Hollywood Studio System: A History, British Film Institute, London.

Figure 6.   The studio system was neither efficient, nor innovative

industry where movies were produced according to fixed and boring patterns and storylines.[27]

This industrial form of organizing of the feature film industry seems archaic for someone who is aware of the working methods of the feature film industry anno 2012 in detail. These days the process of film making begins with an attractive idea, which then turns into a scenario and after that will be sold to the highest bidder. The involved production company may still be a traditional movie studio, but it can also be an independent movie producer. From the moment the producer decides to start with the actual production all the required personnel will be collected from a pool of networks. All the necessary technicians will be hired, a casting agency gets the order to seek actors and actresses, and a director begins directing the movie. The film is then produced by a network of specialists who only comes together during the production of a film. At the end of production phase, the temporary organization will be largely dispersed.

The transition of the Hollywood studio system to a network economy is fascinating for many of today's professional organizations because:

1. With the advent of television, which started around 1950, the demand for cheap and enjoyable TV-films and TV-series was intensified. The small independent producers with their temporary networks proved to be able to create more attractive productions than the traditional big

---

27   Douglas Gomery (2008). A History of Broadcasting in the United States.

studios against a fraction of the costs. The studios struggled against these new independent and agile producers. To the untrained eye, it may be surprising that the studios didn't manage to produce at much lower costs since the studio system was initially organized to produce movies with maximum efficiency; i.e. optimization of the utilization rate was all that mattered.

2. The emergence of this new network type of industry led to more innovative and creative movies. Directors such as Steven Spielberg and Martin Scorsese, and new independent producers such as Jerry Bruckheimer created new blockbuster movies such as 'Jaws' and 'Close Encounters of the Third Kind' and 'Terminator'. At the same time new innovative movies were made by these independent directors such as 'Reservoir dogs' and 'Shadows'. All these movies could not have been made within the old traditional system.

3. The network organization has given more freedom to talented directors to create movies that they want to direct, and for talented actors to play the roles that they want to play. Today it is possible for both actors and directors to work on blockbuster movies alongside their work on independent films. This, on the one hand, will provide much more career satisfaction, and on the other, will cause higher quality and more innovation. It is all because people can follow their own dreams and ambitions.

The feature film industry is a relevant example because it demonstrates the enormous potential of networks. A properly configured network economy is much more efficient and more innovative than any other industrial organizations. Moreover, in a network economy professionals have much more freedom and autonomy to shape their career. No doubt there are also disadvantages to the network way of organizing as is evident in the Hollywood example. First, there is a strong tendency to stereotyping professionals. Since the professional is selected on basis of their past working portfolio, it is hard to give new meaning and direction to their career. Second, there are powerful agents and producers who do not always pursue the interests of the professional. Finally, in the network model scarce resources (e.g. stars) are considerably better paid than widespread resources (e.g. B-actors).

Project based firms
As it discussed in chapter two, due to the ongoing elimination and automation of routine tasks, the modern firm is much more focused on managing changes and accomplishing innovations. The focal point of the modern organization is thus shifting from managing standard tasks to solving complex problems. Hence project-based methods are increasingly used to organize this temporary type of work and solve these intricate

tasks. It is therefore no surprise that the project organization is nowadays ubiquitous. In today's western economy almost every second vacancy is a project position; everyone seems to be a project manager, a project administrator, a project secretary, or a project officer. Although these project organizations can be of any type and size, a key characteristic of these organizations is that they all have a begin and an end. So it is no wonder that Tom Peters argues that the modern firm is nothing more or less than a portfolio of projects.[28] These project-based organizations are defined by of a small center of managers responsible for setting strategic direction, managing clients and suppliers, accompanied by a large collection of professionals who work on temporary projects.

Unfortunately, most of our organizational theories are still based upon the assumption that organizations are permanent. Theories on temporary organizational settings (e.g. project organizations) are still relatively rare. A well-known exception is the theory of Rolf Lundin and Anders Soderholm. They are credited with one of the first scientific frameworks to analyze and understand project organizations.[29] Lundin and Soderholm distinguish two sets of concepts which are essential to understand the essence of project organizations: 1) basic concepts and 2) sequencing concepts. The basic concepts are the foundation for our understanding of the content of projects. The sequencing concepts are the foundation for our understanding of the process and phasing of projects. Everyone who has ever managed a project knows that there are four modules of a project on the content side: task, team, time, and transition. Task is the raison-d'être of the project organization and can be compared to a permanent organization's devotion to goals. It is crucial to understand that a project is a combination of unique and repetitive tasks. If a project organization has a lot of repetitive tasks then to some extent it can be compared to the permanent organizations that focus on efficiency and organizational learning. On the other hand, if the tasks of the project organization are largely unique, other aspects rather than efficiency become central for the success of the project such as vision, flexibility, creativity, dealing with uncertainty, diversity, and determination (Table 2).[30] Team is the second building block of a project. The team in a project is always selected to complete the task at hand. It is not just a randomly selected people. There are two important aspects that define the effectiveness of a team. The first factor is the quality and experience of the project members. Lundin and Soderholm argue that the expectations and experiences of the individual team members provide the basis for commitment and motivation. The trick is to create a team composition

---

28   Tom Peters (1999). The Professional Service Firm 50, Knopf.

29   Rolf Lundin & Anders Soderholm (1995). A Theory Of The Temporary Organization. Scandinavian Journal of Management, 11, 437-455.

30   Nina Modig (2007). A continuum of organizations formed to carry out projects: Temporary and stationary organization forms. International Journal of Project Management, 25, 807–814.

where there is synergy and mutual enforcement of strengths between the members. The second factor is the legitimation of the team and the task at hand, especially with competing teams, the existence of adversaries, or an unresponsive business environment. Do the major stakeholders outside the team understand what the purpose of the team is and how it intends to deliver on its promises? The third defining building block of the project is transition, which is closely related to the task at hand. The purpose of the project is to change something from situation A to situation B. The last essential building block of projects is the time. The element of time is crucial because the lifetime of a project is by definition finite, and because time is often perceived to be somewhat chaotic within projects.

	Repetitive tasks	**Unique tasks**
Goals	Immediate, specified	Visionary, abstract
Experience	Own or codified by professions	Outside or none
Competence	In codes and tacit knowledge	Diverse; requires flexibility and creativity
Control	Management	Leadership
Evaluation	Result orientated	Utility orientated
Learning	Refinement	Renewal

Table 2.   Unique versus repetitive tasks in projects. Based on Lundin and Soderholm

Rolf Lundin and Anders Soderholm argue that the very essence of a project is action. To depict its importance, Rolf Lundin and Anders Soderholm propose that a project contains four standard stages: 1) concept, 2) development, 3) implementation, and 4) termination. Each stage has its own particular tasks, which the team needs to adapt to. In the first phase, a lot of entrepreneurship is needed, while the second phase focuses on building commitment. The third phase concentrates on implementing the task according to the plan, and the final phase requires knowledge transfer. The ideal project organization alters according to the task at hand and the phase of the project.

The framework of Rolf Lundin and Anders Soderholm teaches us something about the essence of projects, but does not provide adequate insights into the organization of the project-based firm (PBF); i.e. a firm exclusively structured to successfully complete various projects in parallel. These days many industries, from construction companies to performing arts, and from architecture to professional services, are in fact PBF's. But an ever growing proportion of the work in traditional industries such as banking, manufacturing, government, and even agriculture are becoming project based. Significant parts of these organizations, for example, the marketing and IT department, are nowadays largely aimed at the successful realization of a portfolio of projects. These departments closely resemble the pure PBF.

But while all the PBF's aim to complete temporary complex tasks by bringing skilled professionals together, they vary considerably in the number and variety of projects they undertake, the customization and appropriability of their deliverables, and the uncertainty involved in achieving their purposes. In this regard, Richard Whitley argues that there are four different types of PBF's and that two dimensions are crucial to discriminate PBF's.[31] The first dimension is the *uniqueness* of deliverables. If deliverables of projects are relatively unique, it is probable that organizations will have to deal with exceptions and adjust their routines. The very nature of deliverables is their limited value of retaining knowledge, which means that an organization is no longer needed after the production. Examples of such industries are feature film productions and complex construction projects where external parties are contracted to work together as a team, but after the completion of the project all parties go their own way. Firms which focus on projects with a high degree of similarity in their outputs may be interested in retaining employees to build firm-specific capabilities. Thus if customers, goals, and problems of projects are comparable it is more important to develop distinctive routines. The second dimension associates with the degree that the professional roles are needed to accomplish the task at hand are properly defined and whether there is a market for such skills. In some industries, like the feature film industry, the roles and skills that are needed to create and deliver a product or service are clearly defined like modules. This modularity of roles enables project teams to come together quickly and cooperate effectively at short notice. New ideas are often developed within these clear-cut roles.[32] Gernot Grabher therefore contends that knowledge in these types of project-based firms is mainly created through changing the team composition, not by developing new ways of working within the team. In other industries the roles within a project are not well defined at all and workers may adopt different roles during the course of a project. Coordination of tasks and skills is a bit more complex in this case, and more time is needed to build a strong team.

Based on these two dimensions (i.e. uniqueness of deliverable and modularity of work roles), Richard Whitley argues that there are four types of PBF's. The first one is the **contractual PBF.** This PBF combines a high uniqueness of deliverables with high modularity of work roles. Feature films and complex construction projects resemble these kinds of PBFs.

31   Richard Whitley (2006). Project-based firms: new organizational form or variations on a theme? Industrial and Corporate Change, 15, 77-99
32   Gernot Grabher (2004). Temporary architectures of learning: knowledge governance in project ecologies, Organization Studies, 25, 1491–1514.

Second is the **craft PBF.** This is a PBF which performs a sizeable number of similar projects and does this with relatively modular skills. Examples can be found in IT where teams of diverse skills are constructed to generate specialist solutions. Expertise and roles in these kinds of PBFs remain quite stable over a series of projects. Typically employees in these craft PBFs owe their primary loyalty to their craft and occupational identity rather than to their current employer. The third type of PBF is the **organizational PBF.** In these PBFs the deliverables across projects are roughly similar; work tends to be repetitive, though work roles are not modular. These kinds of PBFs are quite common in some professional services such as strategic consultancy. As coordination efforts are more difficult than modular PBF's, these PBFs typically develop elaborate procedures for managing knowledge and workflow. Finally, firms contracting skilled staff to work on unique projects can be characterized as **precarious or unstable PBF's.** The combination of unique goals with complex coordination efforts makes these PBF's unstable. Nevertheless these PBF's thrive in certain segments of the market such as incubators and some R&D centers aimed to create a blockbuster drug.

For PBF's which produce unique products and services (i.e. contractor PBF's and precarious PBF's), it is hard to obtain promises and assurances of investors and staff members, especially when the outcome is uncertain due to technological obstacles or market circumstances. Who would want to invest in such a project, and which professionals would want to participate in such a project? For instance, investors in the movie industry are not easily convinced of the attractiveness of a new type of film, just as renowned directors and famous actors, but investors are eager to invest in sequels of blockbuster movies. The risks of a contractor PBF is obviously lower than that of a precarious PBF since the production process, organizational form, capabilities, and roles are predefined. There are standard plans and templates that can be used to distribute, coordinate, and manage the activities.

Studying the four different types of PBF's, one can conclude that the hyperspecialization trend that we signaled earlier indicates the increasing modularity of roles. Moreover, the fact that routine tasks are unquestionably eliminated, even within the projects, presumes that contractor PBF's (e.g. the movie industry) is probably the type of project organization that is most likely to see prolonged growth in the future, followed by growth in craft PBF's and precarious PBF's. The number of organizational PBF's, which in fact may currently represent the largest group of PBF's, will gradually decline in the favor of contractor (e.g. movie), craft (e.g. IT), and precarious (e.g. greenfield ventures) PBF's. Although all kind of projects are becoming relatively more important than the traditional line activities, there are strong trends promoting modularization and singularity.

Uniqueness of deliverables

	Low	High
Low modularity of roles	*Organizational PBFs:* producing multiple and varied outputs with different and changeable skills and roles. *Example:* management consultancy	*Precarious PBFs:* producing unusual outputs with a variety of roles. *Example:* dedicated biotechnology firms, start-up firms
High modularity of roles	*Craft PBFs:* producing multiple, incrementally related outputs with distinct and stable roles and skills. *Examples:* advertising, IT consulting	*Contractor PBFs:* producing single outputs and coordinating tasks through standardized, separate and stable roles and skills. *Example:* complex construction, feature films

Table 3.   Types of Project Based Organization. Source: Whitley (2006)

Overview

1. The new economy is a gig economy. The temporary project organization is the most common form of organization. Organizations have become nothing more or less than a collection or portfolio of projects.

2. History shows that these project forms of organization may lead to more innovative products, more autonomy and happiness of people, and a more efficient production process.

3. Individuals participate in projects, but these individuals are also connected in networks where they share information, create knowledge, and start innovative projects.

4. The importance of the traditional project with repetitive tasks and generic roles is slowly diminishing. In the future project will be unique and/or staffed with specialists. Examples are contractor projects (e.g. movie), craft projects (e.g. software development), and precarious projects (e.g. greenfield ventures).

CHAPTER 5:

THE RISE OF THE SUPERTEMP

66 Why join the navy if you can be a pirate?" Steve Jobs

With the decreasing transaction cost and the changing nature of work, the most logical step for the composition of the workforce is to adapt itself to this new reality. The trends towards specialization and elimination of standard tasks lead to increasing numbers of professionals, i.e. people who are experts in their field and perform a specialized task relatively independently without the supervision of others. Unfortunately it is not very straightforward to estimate the number of professionals in the economy. Steven Barley and Gideon Kunda estimated that in 1960 about eight percent of all US workers could be considered as professionals. This percentage had risen to over twenty percent in 2000.[33] Stephen Herzenberg, John Alic, and Howard Wial similarly estimated the percentage of professionals in the US economy, but their estimation was aimed on the amount of professionals in the service sector.[34] They predicted that approximately 40 percent of all workers in the service sector should nowadays be considered professionals. These numbers indicate that the replacement of routine-workers by professionals is perhaps the biggest shift in the history of the US workforce.

33   Stephen Barley & Gideon Kunda (2006). Gurus, Hired Guns, and Warm Bodies: Itinerant Experts in a Knowledge Economy.
34   Stephen Herzenberg, John Alic and Howard Wial (1998). New Rules for a New Economy: Employment and Opportunity in Postindustrial America, Ithaca: ILR Press.

According to Barley and Kunda, there are four different kinds of professionals: 1) free professions, 2) professional firms, 3) corporate professions, and 4) independent professionals or freelancers. Free professionalism is the oldest form of professionalism. Doctors and lawyers in the 19th and early 20th century are prototypes of this free professionalism. These professionals acquire skills through education and apprenticeships. Once certified they choose a location to practice their craft. Finding clients is relatively easy for these free professionals as almost everyone needs their services at some point in time. The protective regulatory structure that often accompanies these professions guarantees long-term security, although there is often some form of local competition. These industries are often regulated by professional associations and group norms. Regulation also implies that there is no compelling need for continuous education. Particularly in the early days of free professionalism, it was sufficient to remain slightly up to date. Professional firms, such as: law firms, architectural firms and accountancies, cropped up in the beginning of the 20th century. Cooperation allowed the practitioners to specialize, which in turn allowed professional firms to offer a broad scale/scope of services. This process of specialization allowed partners to specialize in client management, whereby junior colleagues performed the actual work. These economies of scale ensured the professional firms to handle more clients at lower costs. In addition, it gave the senior partners a higher income and the junior employee's opportunities to develop themselves. One of the advantages of this form of organization is that it pools expertise and fosters professional development. Corporate professionalism is the third form of organizing professionalism, which turned up up in the beginning of the 20th century, due to economies of scale in industrial organizations. These professionals work as regular employees of firms. Examples of such professionals are: chemists, engineers, lawyers, and accountants. These professionals have no need to market themselves outside their company. The cost for personal development is born by the employer, who pays for education and membership of professional organizations. Sometimes, for instance, in some larger R&D labs, a complete professional community is established within the corporation. Stephen Barley and Gideon Kunda argue that the independent professional or freelancer is a new form of professionalism, which combines elements of traditional approaches with new working traditions. Barley and Kunda write (p.198): *'Like free professionals, these independent professionals worked as solo practitioners and, in most cases, arranged for their own benefits. They drew on professional networks for referrals and recommendations and took responsibility for professional development. Like members of professional firms, they often work for one organization, a staffing agency, but offered their services to another. Like corporate professionals they practice inside organizations, often as members of a team whose work was subject to management direction. But unlike free professionals and members of professional firms, independent professionals are rarely [..] paid on a fee for service basis. Nor were they salaried like corporate professionals or members of professional service firms'.*

The growth of freelancing

Many individuals predict massive growth in the numbers of independent professionals. For instance, according to Gene Zaino, the CEO of MBO Partners, the number of independent workers in the US is currently 16 million people. This number will rise to 65 to 70 million independent workers in the next decade if the current trend is extrapolated.[35] Although these figures may be too optimistic, growth in the number of independent workers seems almost certain. It is quite telling that the movement towards independent professionals is a widespread phenomenon. It is not only in the US, it is also visible in the UK, and in several other Europe countries. In the previous chapters we discussed some of the driving forces behind this expansion. To begin with, diminishing of transaction cost had been a clear contributing factor to the growth of freelancing. Due to internet and mobile telephone the transaction costs of searching, finding, and hiring professionals has decrease significantly. As we speak, software systems are being developed to facilitate searching, finding, collaboration, and cooperation of individuals. Second, the increased standardization of business processes and technology solutions, which led to a significant improvement of professional and industry knowledge over firm-specific knowledge has started the creation of new markets and permitted individuals to go from one assignment to the next. Third, the miniaturization of technology solutions (e.g. databases, design software, 3D-printing) has given the individual much more power. There is no urge to cooperate with others. An individual can nowadays do the job in many professions and sectors, in many cases operating from home without the help of outsiders. Last, but not least, the replacement of repetitive work by temporary projects does fit very well with the temporary nature of freelancing, as we will see later. Temporary jobs are matched with temporary employment contracts. In the past when jobs had a permanent nature, it made sense to match permanent employment with permanent contracts. This is no longer the case. Now there are other factors at play though the mentioned forces are also crucial. For instance, every country has certain institutional influences.

There is, however, one additional factor which determines the attractiveness of solo-entrepreneurship that is often overlooked. It has to do with the changing composition of our economy where individual knowledge and networks are sometimes more important than capital. Benjamin Campbell, Martin Ganco, April Franco, and Rasjree Agarwal looked into the choice

---

35   http://gigaom.com/2011/12/08/mbo-partners-network-2011/

between employeeship and entrepreneurship.[36] They conclude that, the so-called complementary resources, are the most important determinant of entrepreneurship.[37] To explain their arguments one needs to acknowledge that an organization is nothing more than a combination of resources. Some of these resources belong to individuals (e.g. personal networks, tacit knowledge, personal branding), and some belong to the legal entity, the firm (e.g. brand name, machine park). When a person leaves the firm, s/he will take some of these resources with her/his, for instance, tacit knowledge and a network of contacts. But usually the employee is not able to pocket all the valuable resources. A large proportion of the organizational resources remain in the hands of the shareholders such as the brand name, equipment, the client network, tacit knowledge in teams and employees, and explicit knowledge in organizational procedures. These resources are called the complementary resources. When these complementary resources are more valuable than the those of the individual, and if the individual is not able to recreate these resources in one way or another, it is likely that the individual will become an employee, simply because of the lack the necessary resources to produce valuable services or products. But if the value of left behind complementary resources is rather low, or when the individual is able to replace or recreate them, then the chances are high that the individual will become an entrepreneur and a competitor of her/his former employer.

As we discussed earlier, the relative value of complementary resources of firms has been declining lately in favor of the value of human resources. In services, especially in value shops, the unique resources are human and valuable knowledge is tacit. Equipment is no longer irreplaceable as hardware and software have become very inexpensive. Moreover, explicit information is often freely available on the internet. So when these individuals leave, in group or as an individual, the value of the complementary resources is low and can easily be replaced or recreated. In practice, the brand name and the network of contacts are often the only valuable resources that are left behind. Although these resources may sometimes be incredibly valuable, they may be recreated more easily than propriety information and complex production processes. The end result is that it is easy for persons to start a new firm as a solo-entrepreneur or as a partnership. This phenomenon of nascent entrepreneurship is enormously real in value shops such as professional services (e.g. law, accounting, and consulting) and creative businesses where high profile employees leave their firms to form new start-ups. This model of declining complementary

---

36 Benjamin Campbell, Martin Ganco, April Franco and Rajsjree Agarwal (2012). Who leaves, where to, and why worry? employee mobility, entrepreneurship and effects on source firm performance. Strat. Mgmt. J., 33: 65–87.
37 Arjan van den Born (2009). The drivers of career success of the job-hopping professional in the new networked economy - The challenges of being an entrepreneur and an employee, Born To Grow, Amsterdam

assets offers an additional explanation for the growth of freelancers in the service economy. The simple truth is that these individuals do not really need any assets beyond their own skills and networks to add value and be productive. Only when a new person brings in new desired skills, a social personality, and a distinctive network, or if the market puts a premium on more complex services, the freelancer may decide to cooperate with other persons and form a partnership. Collaboration is no longer a necessity for production, but a free choice. In this era, you do not have to work together because the propose of production prescribes it, but you rather work together because you believe it would increase your value and happiness. Your team up method, temporary or permanently, within or without the projects, is largely determined by your own desires and the job requirements.

The long-gone security of employees
Four factors have rapidly reduced the difference between corporate and independent professionals in the last two decades. Firstly, lifelong employee security is no longer an organizational guarantee. The traditional trade-off between employment security and rewards is vanishing in the knowledge economy where demand fluctuates constantly and personnel cost is by far the largest portion of total costs. Security is simply not a valuable promise anymore. Small employers are particularly forced to dismiss employees when demand collapses. The loss of a single large account can sometimes lead to the waves of dismissals. The sources of security and stability are thus rapidly changing. One of the independent professionals in Barley and Kunda's book defines job security as follows: *'Job security is the ability to get a job. Employees don't have job security, because they do not have the networks. They can't call someone and get a job tomorrow morning. They think they have job security, but it's on paper. Real job security is when you have a network [..] that you can simply call and get a job'* (p. 265). This definition by an independent professional highlights the fact that one of the new sources of job security is related to an individuals' social capital and professional capital (or employability). There is no priori reason why the social and professional capital of independent professionals is less than that of employees. Often it is the other way round; through various assignments and having a lot of network contacts, the professional and social capital of independent professionals is higher. Secondly, as turnover rates of managers and employees increase, the employer-employee relationship has also become more formal and transactional. Employees have to prove themselves more frequently and, when they do not perform as expected, the employment relationship comes to an end. This has further reduced job security for employees in comparison with independent professionals. Thirdly, more and more employees have professional careers within organizations. These professionals are typically measured against the same type of yardsticks as freelancers (i.e. billability, project results, et cetera) and they need the same

capabilities. Fourthly, with the arrival of unlimited career the employee has become responsible for managing his/her own career. Organizational career management has increasingly become less important. The employee is not directed to a new position anymore, but he/she needs to direct his own career within or without the organization. This has amplified the importance of networking and further decreased the difference between employment and freelancing. All in all, these four factors contribute to a vanishing difference between employees and independent professionals. The gap between a borderless career worker hopping from job to job every 2 to 3 years and the independent professional leaping from assignment to assignment is not very large. The challenges that they face and the tactics they pursue to resolve their problems are quite alike.

Currently, there are perhaps only three important differences between independent professionals and traditional employees. First of all, an employee still receives some organizational support for continuous personal development, such as: training and networking opportunities. An organization supplies schooling and training opportunities, provides a social network, and offers challenging job opportunities. But Siobhan O'Mahony and Beth Bechky argue that the amount of social support found in external networks can be as much or more than within organizations. [38] There is a continuum between pure free market contracting and structured, guided and supported internal labor markets. In some cases the social support of freelancers is even superior to the organizational support of employees. Secondly, large organizations have the necessary resources (e.g. distribution network, capital, access to specialized knowledge, patents, et cetera) to provide large, complex products and services to clients. These complex assignments provide specific challenges to employees that cannot be replicated easily by freelance networks. This complexity attracts certain types of persons, individuals who excel in the larger bureaucratic environments, those who love to combine technical complexity and challenge (e.g. creating a car) or simply people who love the frequent interactions between colleagues. Thirdly, being an employee still provides a cushion against market forces and temporary misfortunes. In a recession, a company usually first lays off all their peripheral independent professionals before dismissing any of their core employees.

Defining the supertemp
Traditional career theory has always been a theory of stages. For instance, Donald Super argued in the 70s that a career occurs in four stages. [39] Stage one involves exploration and takes place throughout schooling when

---

38 Siobhan O'Mahony & Beth Bechky (2006). Stretchwork: Managing the career progression paradox in external labor markets. Academy of Management Journal, 49, 918-941.
39 Donald Super (1975). Career Education and the Meaning of Work. Columbia University, New York.

career alternatives are considered. Stage two happens when the career is in the early stages of establishment. Stage three includes maintenance and consolidation, where the individuals holds onto their position and continuously update their skills. Stage four contains preparation for disengagement from the workforce. According to Super and Hall a defining moment in the traditional career occurs around the age of 40.[40] After this point, there is continued growth and advancement for some, maintenance and career plateaus for others, and obsolescence, stagnation, and career decline for the third group. The career phase theory of Super and others has received enormous criticism since it lacks empirical validation, but it has been used extensively in organizational practices. Nowadays, all the traditional career theories are treated with doubt and uncertainty, as they do not accommodate the dynamics of new working practices. In the last decades, traditional career theory has been replaced by new views. Recent reformulations of career theory presuppose life course transitions that are multiple and iterative with an emphasis on continuous learning instead of chronological age. Douglas Hall was the first to describe the shift from *'organizational careers'* to *'protean careers'* that are managed by the person, not the single organization.[41] An important feature of the protean career is the sequential process of: 1) change, 2) adjustment and learning (which usually takes 18 months), 3) success, and 4) disaffection and disharmony. These phases can also occur within one job, if the responsibilities and activities change significantly over time. It is obvious that in such a world there is an ardent need for continuous learning.

At the same time, in the early 1990s, another influential career theory was developed in parallel with the protean career theory; the boundaryless career theory by Robert DeFillippi and Michael Arthur.[42] A person with a boundaryless career focuses on crossing career borders. Instead of being dependent on organizational promotions and career paths, he navigates through the continuously changing work landscape. Just as in protean careers, career development is more cyclical with periodical cycles of new skill development rather than career development in traditional careers, which emphasized career stages and ladders. The term boundaryless refers to the fact that the organizational boundaries are becoming less important. Robert DeFillippi and Michael Arthur argue that three classes of variables, referred to as career competencies, determine individual career success in the boundaryless career world. The first career competence of Arthur and DeFillippi's is **Know-why,** which refers to career motivation, personal meaning and identification. This competency is associated with an individual's

---

40   Donald Super & Douglas Hall (1978). Career Development: Exploration and Planning, Annual Review of Psychology, 29, 300-351.

41   Douglas Hall (1976). Careers in organizations, Pacific Palisades: Goodyear.

42   Robert Defillippi & Michael Arthur (1994). The boundaryless career: A competency-based perspective. J. Organiz. Behav., 15, 307–324

capability to understand oneself, to explore different possibilities, and to adapt to constantly changing work situations. The second career competence is **Know-how.** It reflects career-relevant skills and job-related knowledge, which closely relates to established ideas on individual knowledge, skills and abilities. The third, **Know-whom** competence reveals relevant personal and business networks. This refers to career-related networks and contacts, including business relationships and personal connections.

Conducted researches into the career success of freelance professionals have largely substantiated Arthur and DeFillipi success factors of the boundaryless career in the freelance world.[43] The career success of freelancers is largely determined by cyclical and structural market factors (e.g. market transparency), social capital (e.g. network characteristics), and human capital (e.g. generic and professional skills). The relative importance of these factors may vary from profession to profession. These success factors also vary over time and during a career. For instance, the size of a freelancers' network is not very important in economic boom periods when everybody can get an assignment, but network size is definitely very important in periods of economic recession when there is a lack of interesting assignments. Based on these empirical findings and modern contingency theory, a simplified contingency model of freelance success is described below (Figure 7). This model indicates that the success of a freelancer depends on finding an optimal fit (i.e. match) between the demands of the market (i.e. customers) and the capabilities of the freelancer. These freelance capabilities are a) personal capital (know-why), b) professional capital (roughly translated to know-how), and c) entrepreneurial capital (know-

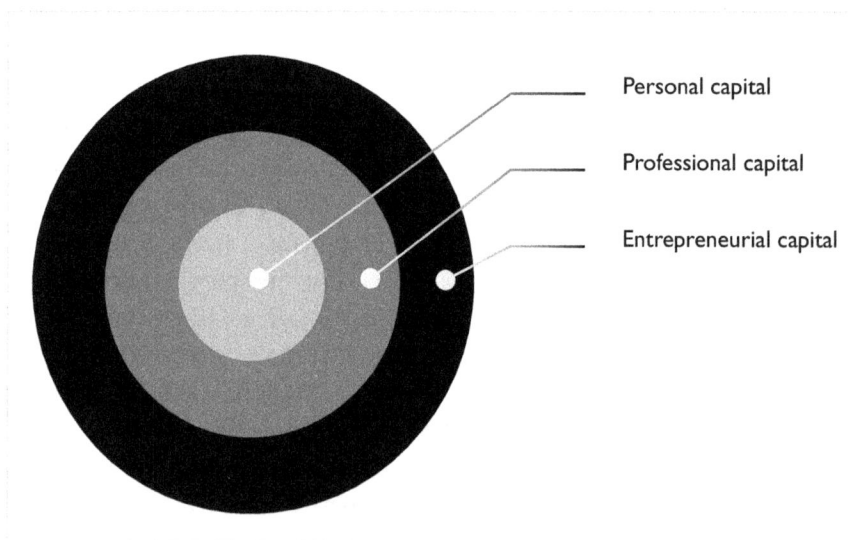

Personal capital

Professional capital

Entrepreneurial capital

Figure 7.   A simple career success model

43   Arjan van den Born & Arjen van Witteloostuijn (2012). Drivers of freelance career success. J. Organiz. Behav. Published online March, 9 2012.

whom). These three clusters of capabilities are still very broadly defined and consist of items such as ambition, motivation, social skills, and personality (personal capital), craftsmanship and knowledge (professional skills), and sales power, reputation, and network characteristics (entrepreneurial skills). [44] The entrepreneurial skills are needed to sell the professional and personal skills to the market and clients. Therefore, the freelancer is a little bit Dr. Jekyll and Mr. Hyde, both entrepreneur and master of crafts.

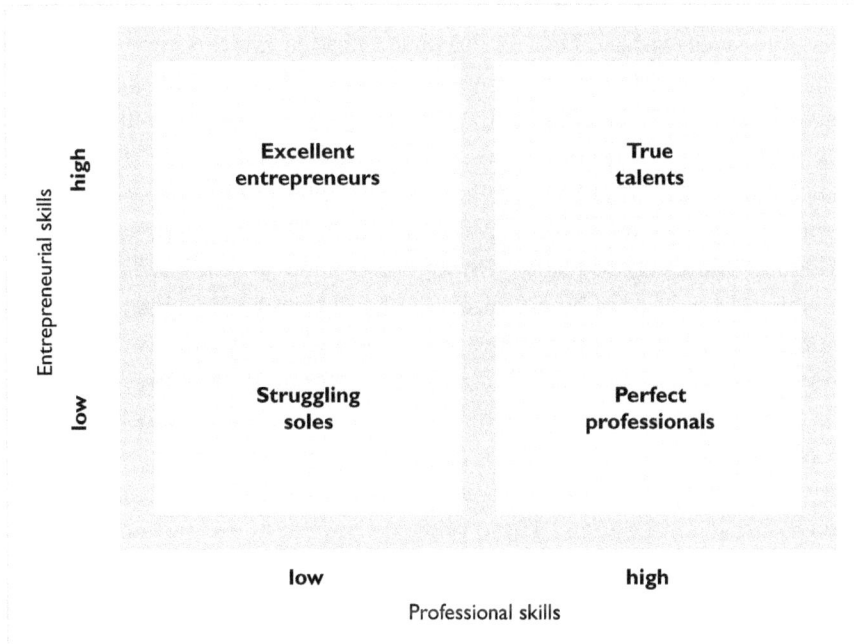

Figure 8. Combining professional and entrepreneurial skills

As indicated, the relative career success factors are dependent on the definition of success but also on the prevailing conditions. In certain situations entrepreneurial skills are more important than professional and personal skills, in other circumstances professional and personal skills are the key to success. This is really dependent on the market, client characteristics, the profession, and the business model of the freelancer. However, two issues are obvious. First, it is crucial that entrepreneurial capabilities are aimed to adjust the external demands with the professional and personal skills of the individual. Second, both entrepreneurial skills and professional skills are important for the future worker. If you lack both skills, you will probably not be very successful. If you master both characteristics you will probably be an acclaimed leader and will be able to demand increasingly higher fees and source less added value work to other freelancers in your network.

---

44 With the large share of services in our economy, cocreationship has become of great importance. Adding value is no longer only about providing factual knowledge, but it is also about the social interaction between outsiders and insiders.

This is depicted in Figure 8 on the previous page depicting entrepreneurial capital versus professional capital.

Those freelancers who lack one of the two skillsets are interesting, i.e. those who lack entrepreneurial skills and the ones who lack professional skills. History teaches us that both types of individuals can still be extremely successful despite this relative lack of skills. There are plenty of examples of successful people with limited entrepreneurial skills and great professional skills and vice versa. This is because various market and product characteristics drive the relative importance of entrepreneurial skills versus professional skills. For example, if you have a service or product that is used quite regularly by your clients, you do not need to find a large client base. What is important is that you create loyal clients by offering them value for money. For such a service or product you do not have to invest a lot in marketing, branding, and sales. On the other hand, if you have a product that is bought only once by a typical client, entrepreneurial skills are quite important as you have to make sure to be found regularly by new clients. Of course, teamwork between individuals who score high on entrepreneurial skills and individuals who score high on professional skills may create the best of both worlds. It is therefore no surprise that such arrangements are quite common. In the world of art, for instance, we see a lot of combinations between artists and agents. These types of combinations are increasingly common in many freelance professions. In fact, the very essence of any prosperous collaboration is perhaps the trick of creating sustainable combinations of professionals with entrepreneurs.

The simplified model of Figure 8 states that the most valuable professionals are those who possess great entrepreneurial skills and are outstanding in their profession as well; they are the true talents. These highly talented individuals will probably make a lot of money as freelancers. It is interesting that these multi-talented individuals are also sought after by firms. Firms increasingly seek individuals that are entrepreneurial and are able to create innovative products and establish new markets. To attract these successful professionals, firms have to be prepared to pay large sums of money or they have to accept other means of collaboration such as partnerships. In this day and age, the firm is not always able to determine the terms of cooperation. As Jody Greenstone Miller and Matt Miller argue in their Harvard Business Review article on the rise of the supertemp: *'Talented people are going independent because they can choose what to work on and with whom to work.'* [45]

---

45   Jody Greenstone Miller & Matt Miller, The Rise of the Supertemp, Harvard Business Review, May 2012.

Overview

1. Independent professionalism or freelancing is a fast growing phenomenon in many western countries.

2. Its growth is primarily driven by technological advancements and changes in the nature of work, although some institutional factors may attribute to this phenomenon as well.

3. Whether an individual becomes an employee or an entrepreneur depends on the complementary assets a firm has to offer. As complementary assets are increasingly found in human networks and skills, it is also logical from this aspect that more professionals chose a freelance career or become partners in a small firm.

4. Independent freelancers who are able to create a match between the market demands and their clients, their personality, professional skills, and entrepreneurial skills will be the winners of tomorrow's economy.

5. Independent freelancers who possess significant professional as well as entrepreneurial skills will be enormously successful. But these multi-skilled individuals will also be preferred by larger firms. To attract these individuals firms have to pay significant wages (above management level). To ensure efficient access to their skills and networks, other arrangements are needed than the traditional employment relationship.

Part II

THE NEW NETWORK FORM OF ORGANIZATION

CHAPTER 6:

MAKE OR BUY

❝ Man has learned to use [the market]…but he is still very far from having learned to make the best use of it."
Friedrich Hayek, The Use of Knowledge in Society, p. 528.

Robert Coase was the first man who thought about the advantages of the market versus organizations.[46] What activities do you insource, and what do you outsource? Since then loads of scholars and theories have contributed to this discussion. Some of these theories such as Transactions Cost Economics (TCE), Resource Based View of the firm (RBV), and the Knowledge Based View of the firm (KBV) will be discussed in this book.[47,48] With the advent of new hybrid forms of organization such as crowdsourcing, the interest for theories separating firm and market is rapidly increasing. In their recent excellent overview of these theories of the firm, Todd Zenger, Teppo Felin, and Lyda Bigelow state the fact that there are many different models which try to explain the boundary of the firm.[49] Some of these models focus on the advantages of markets, other models emphasize the failure of markets. Some models explain why hierarchy is effective for an organization and other models explain why hierarchies tend to fail (Figure 9).

46   Robert Coase (1937). The Nature of the Firm, Economica, 4, 386-405.
47   Oliver Williamson (1975). Markets and hierarchies: analysis and antitrust implications, New York, Free Press.
48   Jay Barney (1991). "Firm resources and sustained competitive advantage", Journal of Management, 17, 99-120.
49   Todd Zenger, Teppo Felin & Lyda Bigelow (2011). Theories of the Firm-Market Boundary. Academy of Management Annals.

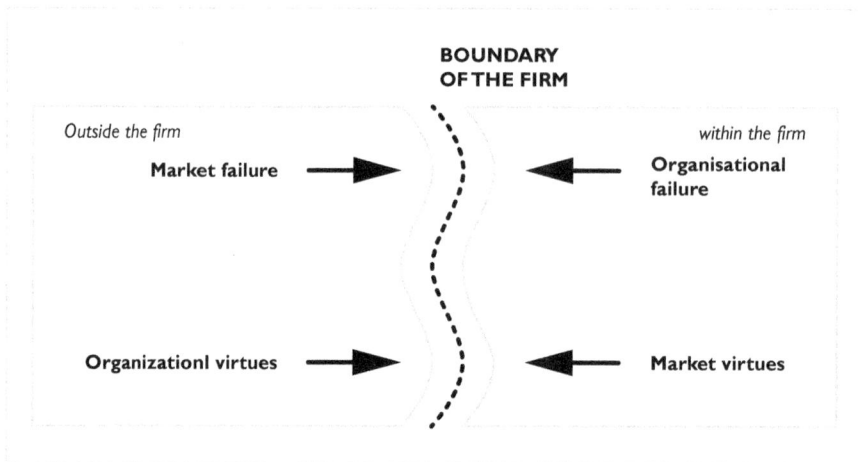

Figure 9.   Markets vs. hierarchies. Source: Zenger, Felin and Bigelow

Zenger, Felin and Bigelow try to answer four relevant questions in their summary of the literature: 1) What are the market's potential advantages? 2) Why and when do markets fail? 3) What are the virtues of organizations as a means of governance? And 4) Why and when do organizations fail? Taken together these four questions explain the border between market and firm.

The advantages of markets

Markets, when they are efficient and if there is no market failure, are powerful means of organization. There are two vital advantages of markets. The first advantage of markets lies in its **ability to effectively match supply and demand.** Although most markets do not adhere to the theoretical ideal of perfect or monopolistic competition, markets tend to be pretty effective and efficient in matching demand and supply while maximizing the value of both participants. To create value, market participants constantly look for capabilities and assets that are complementary to their exiting asset base in order to create value for their customers. Since most products and services are not homogenous, and talent is definitely not a commodity, matching requires market participants to use more information than just prices to guide their decisions. A huge advantage of the market is that it provides market participants with more than one solution. A firm only has to define a particular problem and may invite several suppliers to propose their solutions. The market offers many different options. The second advantage of markets lies in its **capability of producing real-time information.** This constant updating set of information gives buyers and suppliers the right incentives and allows healthy competition to arise. In all of this, price is the pride and joy of markets since they navigate the development of demand and supply. Suppliers enjoy the profit between price received and cost incurred, while consumers appreciate the difference between value received and price paid. Prices thus give valuable information to all market participants about their role and value. High prices attract new competition and low prices put off market entry. Prices are instrumental to competition among (potential) suppliers because they provide strong incentives to suppliers to improve their products, as well as to customers to look for alternatives to obtain value. Thus, effective markets enable healthy competition and provide market participants with the necessary information and incentives to regularly assess whether they add enough value given their capabilities and the evolving needs of customers. Undoubtedly these advantages of markets can only be utilized if there is a set of institutions to govern freedom of exchange and enforcement of contracts. Even effective markets cannot function without some form of governance.[50]

The disadvantages of markets

Before we trumpet the benefits of markets, we should not forget that markets also have many (practical) disadvantages. Fundamentally, a market can only come to life when the benefits of using the market outweigh the costs associated with setting up a market with all the proper (price) information. For certain specific products and services creating a market is simply impossible. Sometimes the number of trades in a certain product or services is just too limited for a real market to emerge. Or in other cases the process of crafting and enforcing contracts is far too costly, especially when contracts cannot be completely specified. The market mechanism is typically **prone to failure when we want to use it to price and trade novel, unique, or very specific products and services.** Moreover, markets are not properly coordinated with several market participants to achieve synergy. Particularly when new knowledge creation requires a complex process of recombination and knowledge transfer, the market mechanism tends to fail as it cannot properly price the value of knowledge assets. **Creating market incentives for knowledge sharing is notoriously difficult** as the right price for information cannot be established without sharing it. However, once the information is shared, the need for payment would vanish.[51] To overcome this problem, other means of collaboration, such as partnerships, need to be established.

The advantages of firms

Organizations have two crucial advantages over markets. The most obvious advantage of the firm is its **clear and unambiguous authority.** Leaders can direct employees to perform specific activities and coordinate the work. This is particularly important in environments that are volatile, uncertain, complex, and ambiguous (VUCA). In such environments, rapid decision making and coordination across different capabilities are crucial. Authority plays then an important role in directing this cooperation and avoiding

50   Douglass North (1990). Institutions, institutional change and economic performance. Cambridge: Cambridge University Press.
51   Kenneth Arrow (1974). The limits of organization. New York: Norton

arguments. A second advantage of firms is that an organization may **build trust and commitment needed to foster cooperation.** In this respect, Janine Nahapiet and Sumantra Ghoshal declare that social capital facilitates the creation of new intellectual capital and that organizations are advantageous to the development of high levels of social capital. It is because of this dense social capital that firms have an advantage over markets in creating and sharing intellectual capital.[52] Firms are not only profit maximizing entities but also social communities. The make-or-buy decision is almost a marriage decision. It signals long term commitment for better or worse. As people have a 'longing to belong' the firm may give employees and other stakeholders a sense of identity and meaning.

	Markets	**Firms**
Advantages	• Ability to effectively match demand and supply across a wide range of options to find the right products and services • Accessing real-time information (prices) to guide behavior and decisions of market participants	• Clear line of authority to coordinate and make decisions • Build high levels of trust to facilitate sharing and cooperation
Disadvantages	• Impossible to use the market to trade specific, unique and novel products and services • The market find it difficult to promote knowledge sharing	• Ego and self-interest lead to sub-optimal decisions • Personal relations hamper optimal decisions • Internal politics may lead to an organizational 'culture of fear' • Need to compare leads to jealousy

Table 4.   Advantages and disadvantages of firms and markets

The disadvantages of firms

Although anyone that has ever worked in organizations instinctively knows the major disadvantages, the causes of organizational failure are relatively under researched. Nevertheless, these disadvantages should be ample, otherwise humankind would end up being employed by a single gigantic firm and the kolkhozes in the former Soviet Union would have been slightly more successful. Zenger, Felin, and Bigelow argue that there are various key behavioral drawbacks of unbounded integration. The first is obvious to all of us: **internal politics.** Leaders and managers in a firm are under pressure of their own egos and self-interest to make suboptimal decisions from an organizational viewpoint. These costs are not always absorbed by the leaders who make these judgments. The second reason for organizational failure can be found in the **social relationships between people.** Many theoretians argue that strong interpersonal relationships are useful to cultivate trust and

---

52   Janine Nahapiet & Sumantra Ghoshal (1998). Social Capital Intellectual Capital And The Organizational Advantage. Academy Of Management Review, 23, 242-266.

The Fuzzy Firm™

cooperation. But there is also a dark side to this as personal relationships may also hamper optimal decision making. Managers may become excessively committed to existing relationships beyond what is economically sound. There is a significant risk of over-embeddedness. However, it should be noted that most firms, contrary to what organizational theoritians believe, are not very well known for their high levels of trust. At times organizational politics lead to an organizational culture where fear and anxiety are the norm, not trust and cooperation.[53] The last drawback of firms lies in our human natural urge to compare ourselves. All humans **compare their rewards to others' and react negatively** to perceived inequities. Because people like to compare themselves to those with greater rewards, they tend to exaggerate their personal contribution, and because the real contribution is often subjective, this means that people often feel they are undervalued and unappreciated. In a firm there are always disputes about the rewards and employees are easily displeased and annoyed. In the best case this would result in low morale and high employee turnover. In the worst case scenario this discontentment would result in decreasing efforts, sabotage, and political behavior by managers and employees. It is thus clear that a big potential advantage of the market is that its prices are considered to be more objective and therefore individuals perceive this reward as fair.

Make or buy: traditional sourcing

In the past these advantages and disadvantages where translates in strategic sourcing models which determined what a company should do and what should be outsourced. A good example of such a (traditional) sourcing model is that of Mark Gottfredson, Rudy Puryear, and Stephen Phillips.[54] The title of their article ('*Strategic Sourcing – from Periphery to the Core*') demonstrates that organizations are increasingly outsourcing their core activities. The question whether an organization possesses a certain competence is no longer relevant. It is much more relevant if the organization can get hold of this competence when is need. Crucial resources should be available within the network, not necessarily within the boundaries of the organization. It should be available 'in the cloud'. The authors propose a simple two-step plan to determine whether a particular activity should be outsourced or not. Step one is to determine the real core of the business. Whether an activity is core to an organization is determined by two aspects. The first aspect is the **intrinsic value** of the activity which is determined on the basis of two questions: 1) do we deliver more added value to customers than the competition through this activity?, and 2) what is the strategic damage if competitors can imitate this activity accurately? The second aspect is the

53 Bernd Kriegesmann, Thomas Kley & Markus Schwering (2005). Creative errors and heroic failures: capturing their innovative potential, Journal of Business Strategy, 26, 57 - 64
54 Mark Gottfredson, Rudy Puryear & Stephen Phillips (2005). Strategic Sourcing from Periphery to the Core, Harvard Business Review, 83, 132-139

uniqueness of the activity. Is the activity unique to the firm and the sector or is it generic? Both aspects are then plotted in a matrix (Figure 10) to determine outsourcing potential. Generic activities with a low intrinsic value can be outsourced and organization-specific activities with a high intrinsic value are kept in house. The second step is then to determine the effectiveness and efficiency of the activities. If an activity is carried out efficiently and with high quality, it may be wise to set up a new company, if the activity is not of strategic value to the firm.

The model of Gottfredson, Puryear, and Philips is quite representative of traditional models governing outsource decisions. In all of these models the core of a company is first determined on the basis of added value and potential strategic damage.[55] Then these models examine the impact of outsourcing on efficiency and effectiveness. If an activity is not considered strategically important and if it is not performed efficiently or effectively, outsourcing would be the logical consequence. In such models, the outsourcing decisions is binominal; either you outsource an activity or you do it yourself.

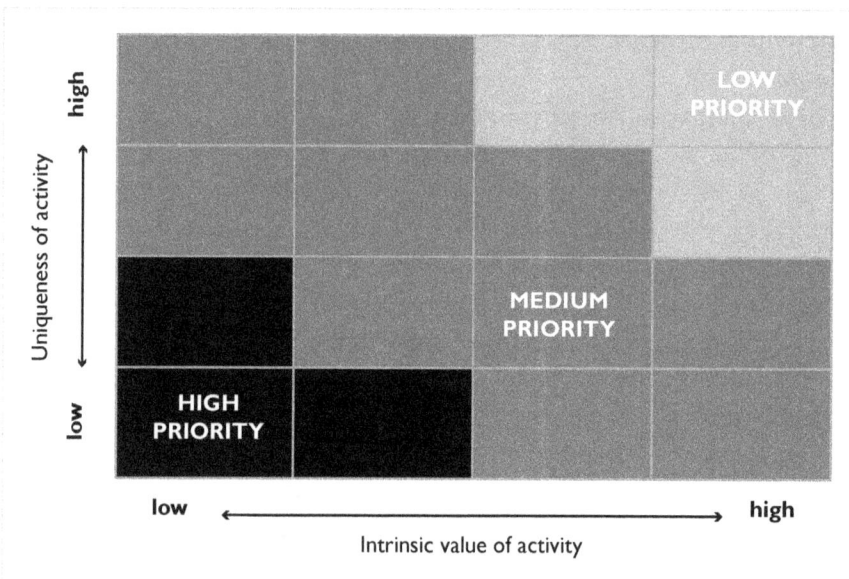

Figure 10. Outsourcing in traditional make-or-buy decisions

55 Ronan McIvor (2008). What is the right outsourcing strategy for your process?. European Management Journal, 26, 24-34.

Overview

1. Work is traditionally governed by either firms or markets. Both forms of governance have specific advantages.

2. Markets excel in the availability of real-time information to guide behavior and decisions and the ability to effectively match demand and supply. But it is impossible to use the market in case of specific, unique, and novel services.

3. Firms stand out when authority is required to make complex and fast decisions and high levels of trust is desired to facilitate sharing and cooperation. But ego, self-interest, and strong personal relations may lead to suboptimal decisions. People instinctively need to compare themselves with others that often leads to an unproductive feeling of jealousy. In more extreme cases, it may even lead the internal politics to an organizational 'culture of fear'.

4. Traditional outsourcing models focus on the make-or-buy decision. The make-or-buy decision is determined by strategic value, efficiency, and effectiveness. Such models are binominal whether or not you outsource an activity.

CHAPTER 7

NEW FORMS OF COLLABORATION

66 A firm will contract until the cost of carrying out an extra transaction on the open market becomes equal to the costs of organizing the same transaction within the firm." The inverse of Robert Coase's Law

In the last chapter we have discussed the advantages of markets and firms and considered traditional sourcing models that determine if an activity should be insourced or outsourced. But increasingly we understand that these models have two disadvantages. First, traditional sourcing models have a static character and emphasize the optimal decisions given the current situation. Such models are thus not very applicable to the real-life dynamic, fast-changing world in which we live. Second these traditional sourcing models are binary; they do not allow for mixed, hybrid or network forms of government where activities are partly outsourced and governance is shared between partners.

Outsourcing; a dynamic perspective

New sourcing models such as those of Sharon Matusik and Charles Hill emphasize the great dynamism in today's society.[56] In their model, two variables determine whether an organization should use outside expertise. The first variable is the extent to which the environment is characterized by extreme competition, resulting in strong cost pressure, and rapidly

---

56   Sharon Matusik & Charles Hill (1998). The Utilization of Contingent Work, Knowledge Creation, and
       Competitive Advantage, The Academy of Management Review, 23, 680-697

changing economic circumstances. Flexibility is of great importance in these markets. The second variable is the forces at work of the environment, in particular the speed of technological development. Dynamic environments are generally characterized by rapid technological change, short product life cycles, and a Schumpeterian process of innovation and creative destruction. In such an environment, it is important to improve the quality of the permanent staff continuously. Not only by serious investing in training and knowledge development, but also by confronting the permanent staff with the outsiders frequently. (Table 5)

Sharon Matusik and Charles Hill argue that there is such thing as an optimal dose of organizational flexibility. Depending on the market in which an organization operates there is an optimal numerical flexibility (which is determined by competition, cost pressures, and economic cycles) and an optimal functional flexibility (determined by dynamics and renewal of the environment). This approach supplements the traditional sourcing models since it indicates the presence of the optimal level of outsourcing dependent of the environment of the business.

	Environment	
	Stable	Dynamic
Mild competition and cost pressures	• Knowledge preservation is important • Knowledge development is relatively unimportant • Cost savings is relatively unimportant	• Knowledge preservation is relatively unimportant • Knowledge development is important • Cost savings is relatively unimportant
Intense competition and cost pressure	• Knowledge preservation is important • Knowledge development is relatively unimportant • Cost savings is important	• Knowledge preservation is relatively unimportant • Knowledge development is important • Cost savings is important

Table 5.   The dynamic model of Matusik and Hill

Outsourcing knowledge; make, buy, or ally

The traditional make-or-buy decision states that companies should focus on those activities that are of strategic importance and which offer a competitive advantage. All other activities should ideally be outsourced to the market. Unfortunately, this simple make-or-buy decision no longer applies to the new gig economy. The uncomplicated make-or-buy decision is increasingly transforming itself into a very difficult make-buy-and-ally decision. This increased complexity has primarily to do with the difficulty of outsourcing knowledge. There are five different reasons why knowledge cannot be easily outsourced:

1. Knowledge sits in the mind. Such tacit knowledge is by definition not easy to copy. According to Sidney Winter such knowledge is also an important source of competitive advantage and therefore something you don't like to outsource. [57] Even if you would want to outsource such activities, this is typically associated with the transfer of a significant part of the employees as the professional knowledge is hardwired in the minds of these people.

2. Knowledge-intensive services cannot be outsourced completely. Even if you would like to outsource a certain activity, because you are pretty terrible in it, the chances are that you cannot outsource a knowledge intensive activity. The simple truth is that input of your organization remains crucial for a beneficial solution to the problem. [58]

3. To solve a problem it is often necessary that all parties involved in the solution share a common understanding of context.[59] Information can be worthless and meaningless if people do not understand the proper context in which the information is positioned. This context has many dimensions such as industry, profession, and organization. If an external party does not really understand and appreciate this context, it will not recognize the real underlying value of the available information. This would make it challenging to outsource activities to parties which do not really understand the context.

4. There is never a promise of success in knowledge work. Knowledge is not an industrial product that consists of a fixed number of ingredients that, according to an organized prearranged production process, will ultimately lead to certain outcomes. The precise outcome of knowledge production is highly unpredictable, like the position and speed of quarks. This would make it awkward to outsource such activities. Not only because there is an inherent risk that the performance would be deficient, but also because there is a chance that the performance would be much greater than imagined, which would lead to appropriability problems (e.g. who gets the reward?).

5. It is almost impossible to reverse outsourcing decisions. Once knowledge is gone astray, it requires much more effort to obtain it.

This all means that attracting and transferring knowledge is pretty costly, thereby making outsourcing of knowledge activities generally an unattractive proposition. The costs of knowledge transfer can be limited, if the knowledge involved is explicit. However,, if the knowledge resides mainly in the minds of people, the transfer costs may be sky-high. Luckily there is a third type of knowledge between tacit and explicit knowledge,

57 Sidney Winter (1987). Knowledge and competence as strategic assets, Handbook on Knowledge Management, 1, 159-184

58 Lance Bettencourt, Amy Ostrom, Stephen Brown & Robert Roundtree (2002). Client Co-Production in Knowledge-Intensive Business Services. California Management Review, 44, 100-128.

59 Burkhart Holzner (1968). Reality construction in society, Schenkman, Cambridge, Mass.

namely when knowledge is encrypted or certified. This type of knowledge can be traced in many professions. Professional associations have typically a well-defined body of knowledge (BOK) which determines which type and level of knowledge can be expected of a professional in a certain area with a certain degree.

Given the above theoretical problems with outsourcing knowledge-intensive activities it is not surprising that Arup Sen and Alan McPherson conclude that outsourcing knowledge-intensive activities often lead to increases in costs, coordination efforts, and a lower quality of service.[60] Moreover, although an organization which obtains its knowledge from outsourcing partners may be more efficient, but its knowledge development capabilities tend to decrease rapidly. In the end this would lead to a lower level of entrepreneurship as outsourcing has negative consequences for seeing and seizing opportunities in the market. Ultimately this leads to lower performance of such firms.[61] Where standard processes can be outsourced with reasonable degrees of success, the outsourcing of knowledge activities is much more complex.

Although outsourcing of knowledge-intensive services is difficult, there are also great potential advantages if one is able to outsource activities in an intelligent way. First, outsourcing would lead to more financial, numerical, and functional flexibility for firms. As we have seen, flexibility is of major importance in the dynamic and competitive gig economy. Second, through outsourcing firms can realize and guarantee long-term access to scarce specialist knowledge. This is becoming more important with increasing specialization across value configurations where even huge organizations are much too small to have all the necessary specialists in-house. Third, innovation had increasingly become important and genuine innovation requires combining new competences and different people. Some of these people reside in the traditional organizations while some remain outsiders.

Although it is almost impossible to outsource knowledge-intensive processes successfully, it has become very difficult to innovate and develop products and processes in-house without the support of outsiders. The tendency towards specialization indicates that organizations which have all-purpose skill employees will not be able to compete against the networks of specialists. In other words, it requires too much time and money to train generalists to fulfill specialist tasks, and the result would be inadequate. In the future problems will be more complex, as we have automated routine

---

60   Arup Senand & Alan MacPherson (2009). Outsourcing, external collaboration, and innovation among U.S. firms in the bio-pharmaceutical industry. The Industrial Geographer, 6.
61   Carmen Weigelt (2009). The impact of outsourcing new technologies on integrative capabilities and performance, Strategic Management Journal, 30, 595–616.

problems, and integration of different viewpoints is thus necessary to solve them. This, however, requires an open attitude and teamwork between various partners to stay ahead[62].

A new sourcing model; collaboration

We have seen that there is a classic 'make-or-buy' decision for tangible products and routine services, but with knowledge-intensive services there is a 'make-buy-or-ally' decision where a form of partnership often seems to be the best solution.[63] Through collaboration you take advantage of the most qualified people and the best resources outside of your organization to improve the quality of products and services and you are able to contain the costs and risks associated with outsourcing.[64] Through collaboration an organization makes sure to obtain permanent access to specific knowledge and safeguard the continual development of that knowledge. Moreover, through cooperation organizations may offer products and services to customers which they cannot produce economically on their own.[65]

Seeing it all, should the organization of the future outsource knowledge services? There is no immediate yes or no answer, because it depends on the amount of change or turbulence in the environment and the type of knowledge needed for the creation of services, products, and new ideas. There are several reasons why the turbulence is an important factor. We saw from Sharon Matusik and Charles Hill that it is important to be numerical, financial, and functional flexible. It is more than just coping with high levels of competition, because an organization constantly needs to adjust itself to the fluctuations of the environment. In such instable environment an organization may not be able to train and develop internal knowledge, and consequently will need to obtain knowledge from outside. The organization needs to renew its resources. And finally there is perhaps a third and even more important reason why the level of change determines the allure of outsourcing. It can be found in the art of creativity. To be truly innovative and resourceful, an organization may need to incorporate outside viewpoints and promote intense alliance with the outsiders. Whether or not an organization should outsource also depends on the type of knowledge needed to solve a particular problem. If this knowledge is very organizational specific, it simply cannot be outsourced. But other forms of knowledge such as professional and generic skills may be outsourced, just as the traditional

---

62 Problems vary in structure (i.e. what knowledge is necessary to solve a problem) and complexity (i.e. the interdependencies between the various areas of knowledge). See Jack Nickerson & Todd Zenger (2004). A Knowledge-Based Theory of the Firm - The Problem-Solving Perspective. Organizational Science, 15, 617-632.
63 Paul Adler, Charles Heckscher & Laurence Prusak (2011). Building a Collaborative Enterprise. Harvard Business Review, July-August.
64 Susan Mudambi & Stephen Tallman (2010). Make, Buy or Ally? Theoretical Perspectives on Knowledge Process Outsourcing through Alliances. Journal of Management Studies, 47, 1434–1456.
65 Christos Pitelis & David Teece (2009). The (new) nature and essence of the firm. European Management Review, 6, 5–15.

outsourcing literature suggests. These arguments are depicted in Figure 11. The figure shows that markets should only be used in environments that are characterized by continuous renewal and strong business fluctuations and where organizational specific knowledge is not that important. The long-term employer-employee relationship is especially relevant in the businesses that have a steady market and business that require very specific knowledge.

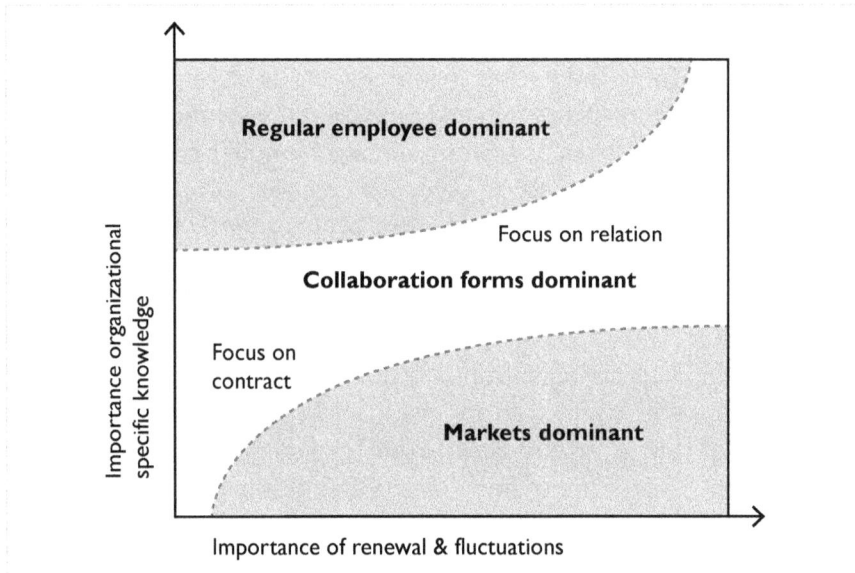

Figure 11. Make, buy or ally in the 21st century

Of course, there are many forms of teamwork. Just think of alliances, cooperatives, partnerships, and joint ventures. One can make a distinction between alliances which emphasize on contractual conditions and partnerships focusing on relationship and trust. The first mode of collaboration will only function if the knowledge of the partner-organization is largely complementary to the knowledge of the organization and if the knowledge can be somewhat encrypted. Then such an outsourcing arrangement, which is very similar to traditional outsourcing and subcontracting relationships, may be used. In the second mode of cooperation trust and long-term relationships are much more crucial. These soft modes of cooperation are especially relevant if the outsourced capability is essential to the core processes of the organization and if that knowledge is largely tacit.

Combining these two dimensions (turbulence and required knowledge), will create the following six different possible solutions for the 'make-buy-or-ally' decision (Figure 12):

1. **Command.** This hierarchical solution is most favorable if control and decisiveness are needed, the necessary knowledge can be found in the

heads of people in the organization and creativity and innovation are trivial.

2. **Cells.** This solution is optimal if creativity and innovation are looked-for and all the necessary specialist knowledge can be found in the heads of the employees of the organization.

3. **Coalitions.** This solution is most selected if control and risk management are crucial, but the required knowledge is only partly in the heads of people in the organization. Employees have to work together with outside organizations in coalitions or alliances.

4. **Communities.** This solution is optimal if profound professional knowledge and creativity are both indispensable and the necessary knowledge can partly be found outside the organization.

5. **Contracts.** This solution is the best if both control and cost control are needed and the necessary knowledge is largely generic and/or supplementary to the knowledge available within the organization.

6. **Crowds.** This solution is optimal if professional knowledge and creativity are needed and the necessary knowledge is largely generic and/or supplementary to the knowledge available within the organization.

	Make	Collaborate	Buy
Create	Cells	Communities	Crowds
Control	Command	Coalitions	Contracts

Figure 12. New forms of knowledge governance

Usually different sets of knowledge are required to solve a certain problem. For instance, to innovate, organizational and professional knowledge are often both needed to identify and implement new solutions. This knowledge can be found in communities or at certain alliance partners. But at the same time perhaps thorough understanding of the design of the current processes is required, as well as the method with which these processes are actually being executed. Such information may require organizational knowledge. This indicates that a typical problem may require different sets of knowledge and therefore different sources of that particular knowledge.

New hybrid forms of governance

In the above we have seen that novel combinations of market and firm are emerging. However, there are two important issues that require consideration. First, these so-called hybrid solutions will have specific drawbacks too. Second, many governance modes are already in practice combinations of pure markets and firms. Sometimes there are strong interrelations between individuals in markets. Some long-term alliances may in reality closely resemble firms. Despite these two shortcomings, we can agree that hybrid forms of governance have indeed the potential to be the best of both worlds. Infusing price information and co-creating knowledge markets may improve the effectiveness of the firms. And fostering trust amongst market participants will improve the long-term effectiveness of the markets. Candace Jones, William Hesterly, and Stephen Borgatti have identified four conditions which are necessary for these hybrid modes of governance to flourish: 1) demand uncertainty with stable supply, 2) high human asset specificity, 3) complex tasks under time pressure, and 4) frequent exchanges among parties comprising the network.[66] Where demand uncertainty and task complexity both favor a market (i.e. contracting) style of governance, asset specificity and frequency of exchange favor a hierarchical style of governance. If a combination of these opposing forces is present in an industry, the result is often a hybrid form of governance.

The advice of Jones, Hesterly, and Borgatti on hybrid modes of governance is becoming more and more valuable as new technological developments have increased our possibilities to infuse market-related solutions into firms. Crowdsourcing and communities are examples of such market-type solutions. Moreover, with the decreasing transaction costs and recent possibilities, market-type solutions have become more interesting. This would enable firms to look for hybrid forms of governance and use markets and hierarchies more in parallel.

---

66   Candace Jones, William Hesterly & Stephen Borgatti (1997). A General Theory of Network Governance: Exchange Conditions and Social Mechanisms, The Academy of Management Review, 22, 911-945.

Overview

1. New dynamic models show that flexible relationships, outsourcing, and collaboration with the outside partners are strategically significant in environments which are coping with extreme competition, rapidly changing economic circumstances and fast technological development.

2. It is much harder to outsource knowledge services than routine services. The simple make-or-buy decision no longer applies and it has turned to a make-buy-and-ally decision where modes of collaboration and cooperation dominate.

3. New hybrid or network solutions where elements of markets and firms are mixed, such as communities and crowdsourcing, are promising and gaining market share.

4. Firms are also using markets as well as hierarchy as competing modes of governing relations. This enables companies to benchmark both methods. With the arrival of social media and the internet new outsourcing options such as communities and crowds have emerged. These outsourcing options tend to be very attractive in dynamic environments where innovation and knowledge development are more important than control and knowledge protection.

CHAPTER 8:

THE FUZZY FIRM

66 There is nothing worse than a sharp image of a fuzzy concept." Ansel Adams

In this chapter, as we describe the outline of the firm of the future. All our arguments in the previous sections will come together. We have seen that the economy is changing rapidly into an economy structured around projects, assignments or 'gigs'. To complete these 'gigs' effectively, knowledge and networks are rapidly becoming the foremost production factors; far more important than the traditional factors of capital and labor. The workers themselves are also subject to change. They are no longer routine laborers but have transformed themselves into skilled and trained professionals (independent or not) who are exceptionally knowledgeable in a certain, specialist field of expertise and/or have access to a network of suppliers and clients. What do all these immense changes in work and workers exactly mean for tomorrow's firm?

From hierarchy to network

In chapter four we discussed that the charm of markets as a mode of governance is rising as a result of the decreasing technological costs. The advance of technology (i.e. internet, data analytics, social media, and mobile) creates a shift towards market style elements in the way firms obtain, maintain, develop, and control knowledge capabilities; networks of hyperspecialist firms are emerging and rapidly replacing the traditional hierarchy (Figure 13). Moreover, the same technology developments also create a shift in work where routine activities are rapidly eliminated or outsourced leaving knowledge intensive and creative work to be performed by humans.

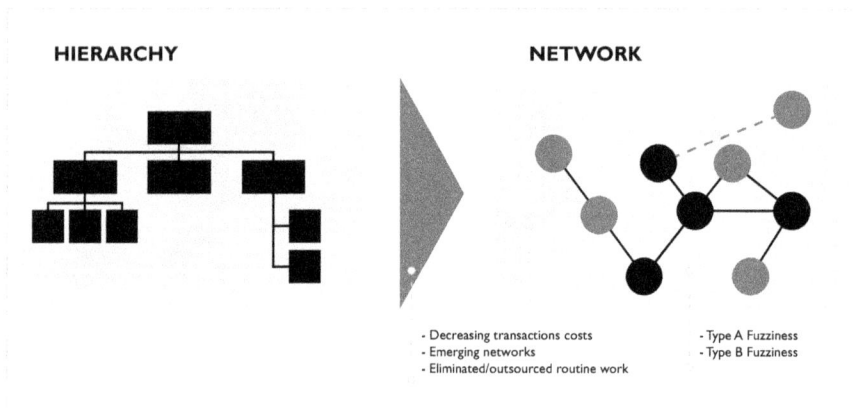

Figure 13. From Hierarchy to Fuzzy Firm

Obviously, not all routine activities will disappear overnight. Moreover, the fact that these activities and processes are not performed by humans (but by computers and hence are called IT or process services) does not imply that firms cannot make money from routine activities. Far from it, large corporations in every field are demonstrating every day that one can make a lot of money from routine work. From consumer goods to banking and from utilities to networks, large corporations are making a lot of money from performing routine work efficiently and effectively and this exploiting earlier inventions. In order to exploit these earlier inventions requires major financial investments in IT and distribution power as these activities and processes often exhibit significant economies of scale and scope.

With the decomposition of traditional value chains, value networks and value chops and the resulting emergence of networks of hyperspecialists, some large generalists run the risk of becoming obsolescent. They just cannot provide the same quality at the low cost. Hyper specialists can produce two times higher quality in a considerably shorter period of time. Hyper specialists pick and find niches in the knowledge intensive service sector and offer a much better price-quality ratio than the larger firms. However, this does not imply that larger firms are not needed in the future. On the contrary, there are significant economies of scale in many markets, as explained above, and generalist with distribution and marketing power are needed. These firms are the ones who connect the dots between hyper specialists. They are the centers of gravity in the network; i.e. the nucleus firms. In network sectors, such as the construction or the feature film industries, such firms supervise the cooperation between various parties. In the feature film industry they are called producers, while in the construction industry they are known as project development companies. These firms are the main contracting parties and work with various subcontractors to get the job done. Their ultimate responsibility is to deliver the assignment. They are also the main financial beneficiary of residual profits, and take on board a significant portion of the risk. In short we witness the emergency of new ecosystems consisting out of small hyperspecialist firms (type A firms) and larger generalist firms (type B firms).

Although both firms are poles apart with different roles in the ecosystem, both firms demonstrate fuzzy characteristics. Type A firms (specialists) will typically focus on production and/or innovation of both products and services. In many cases these firms sell their products and services to the Type B firms (generalists). In order to remain competitive they need to innovate. So as to innovate these Type A firms need specialized domain-relevant skills, but at the same time they need to interact and work with various outside specialist to bring in new perspectives and they need to constantly hire new talents. They will continuously try to improve their products and develop new markets. In order to do so they will have various projects where insiders and outsiders collaborate. The type B firm also demonstrates fuzzy characteristics. First, a significant part of production and innovation of these firms will be outsourced, making it difficult to determine the boundaries between the generalists and the networks of specialists. Second these firms will continuously try to improve their products they bring to their consumers. To protect their position they will need to integrate new innovations as soon as possible into their product or service portfolio. As we will see later, these firms do not pursue a traditional R&D strategy, but rather an Acquisition and Development (A&D) strategy.[67] Such as A&D strategy allows these Type B firms to profit from inventions elsewhere in the value network, and at the same time limits the risk of losing competitive advantage.

To fulfill the coordinating, commanding, contracting, and controlling role of Type B firms, these nuclear organizations have to: 1) be customer-focused and have a service attitude to create loyal customers, 2) plan, organize, and lead projects/services, 3) manage the risks of projects/services, and 4) manage their network, i.e. selecting the right people and resources (subcontractors). Firms that are capable of performing this central role in networks are able to connect a continuously changing network of suppliers and clients to one another. The overall network typically consists of both employees of the focal firm and a range of external suppliers as well as clients. The network can be considered fuzzy because it expands and contracts with new nodes from project to project and from phase to phase. And within the projects it is

---

67   Michel Ferrary (2011). Specialized organizations and ambidextrous clusters in the open innovation paradigm, European Management Journal, 29, 3, 181.

very hard to separate employees from outside contractors. The optimal mix between internal employees and outside partners changes continuously and it depends on a number of factors, such as the phase of the project.

In reality one may see organization which mix Type A with Type B characteristics. These firms are also known as ambidextrous firms as they focus both on exploitation and exploration.[68] A possible structure for a Type B firm is to hold controlling stakes in a certain number of Type A firms. The advantages are clear, through the knowledge of Type A firms, it is easier to understand the market and the innovations in that market. Such an ownership structure could be structured in many ways. This effectively makes the Type B firm an venture capitalist (e.g. in pharma) or even an talent developer (in the case of the arts). As seen from this example the structures of fuzzy firms vary radically. In certain circumstances the firm may well be an old-fashioned partner structure similar to some accounting and law firms. The structure may be a cooperative one such as Mondragon, or even a corporation with limited ownership for some or all the partners. Sometimes these firms have a solid core of professionals with longstanding relationships with both the firm and each other. In the academic world you would say that these professionals have tenured. But many other contracts with professionals will be flexible. This is partly because flexible arrangements provide more career possibilities to the individual professional, but also because boutiques cannot really guarantee long-term contracts. Such promises will only be considered as void since a slight fluctuation in demand will have a direct impact on the cost structure of such a firm. Since all the costs of professional firms are labor costs, and because fixed costs are very limited, fluctuations in demand will immediately lead to adjustments in headcount. Hyperspecialists have a high need for functional and numerical flexibility.

The idea that the firm is becoming fuzzy only applies to the ever-changing boundaries of the firm. In contrast, both the identity and the legitimation of the fuzzy firm are becoming stronger and more pure than most of today's organizations. In order to stand out within the network and to attract clients as well as contractors, the fuzzy firm needs a distinct identity. This essence of the firm cannot change too much because then there will be the risk the alienation of the corresponding network. It may be compared with a sports association such as a football club where the constant renewal of players does not really undermine the identity and legitimation of the club. But if the club decides to relocate to another city (like the Brooklyn Dodgers) or pursues a new sport (say baseball instead of football), its survival would

68   James G. March (1991). Exploration and exploitation in organizational learning, Organization Science, 2, 71-87.

be at stake since such a change would defy the identity of its staff and the legitimation of its position in the network (e.g. supporters).

Case: GlaxoSmithKline

The business model of large pharmaceutical companies has always been based on promotion on the one hand, and R&D, on the other. This model was extremely successful until 1990s. Growth and profits were higher than in most other industries. But since the mid-1990s, all this changed and the traditional growth model came under great pressure. Profitable patents were expired and new patents were not adequate to replace these blockbusters. This resulted in great pressure on R&D to advance more efficiently and effectively. To create a more efficient and effective R&D organization GlaxoSmithKline (GSK) has split its large R&D organization into many small Centers of Excellence. The old hierarchical pyramid is now a network of independent cells. These cells are increasingly working together with external parties. They join forces with the best companies and universities on different areas of competence. Each Center of Excellence may decide its own make-or-buy strategy. Each Center of Excellence may also decide how to cooperate. GSK has also external Centers of Excellence for Drug Discovery. There are teams of about 25 people within GSK who are focused on contracting with external parties.

This open architecture has many advantages according to GSK. It allows internal and external competitions among different methods and makes the organization much more flexible. Projects can be stopped without painful restructuring. But this new form of structured network also means that GSK has to create new capabilities (e.g. how to evaluate projects or set up and manage various partnerships ?).

The transition to fuzzy firms

Currently we are in a transition phase where large firms are increasingly under pressure of newcomers who specialize on a certain aspect of the value chain. Routine work is automated and eliminated or outsourced to hyperspecialists. But as we have seen, it is hard to outsource innovative knowledge work. For these activities organizations are looking for old and new collaborative structures between internals and externals. For instance to staff the portfolio of temporary projects, firms source the required (specialized) knowledge through various channels. Some knowledge (i.e. organizational specific) will still be obtained in-house, but a substantial share of additional professional knowledge will be sourced through the use of hybrid and external networks. This trend towards sourcing through outside networks is fuelled by a number of factors. First, all work becomes temporary work. It therefore makes sense to match temporary work with temporary skills. Second, market-type solutions are becoming an increasingly attractive alternative to hierarchies. Hybrid and dual modes of governance are particularly appealing. Third, the declining importance of organizational specific knowledge in combination with the swollen importance of professional skills is creating new markets of professionals. Fourth, flexibility is becoming more important as global competition increases and the rate of technological development remains high. Particularly, in services where labor costs represent the large majority of all costs, it is crucial to have flexible labor costs. It is important to be able to shed capabilities and resources fast when the workload of the project portfolio diminishes and to attract new capabilities and resources when the project portfolio extends.

As we have seen in chapter five, during this transition process many valuable and rare talents will leave the firm to start their own firms with or without partners. These entrepreneurs use their knowledge and networks to invent new value propositions to new or existing markets. Sometimes they start competing with their former employer, but in most cases they start firms which contribute to the value proposition of their former employer thereby augmenting the ecosystem of the old parent firm. Typically these new firms are initially much smaller than the parent firm focusing on a specialized niche. The parent firm will slowly transform itself from a hierarchy to a fuzzy firm; where the traditional boundaries are rapidly disappearing.

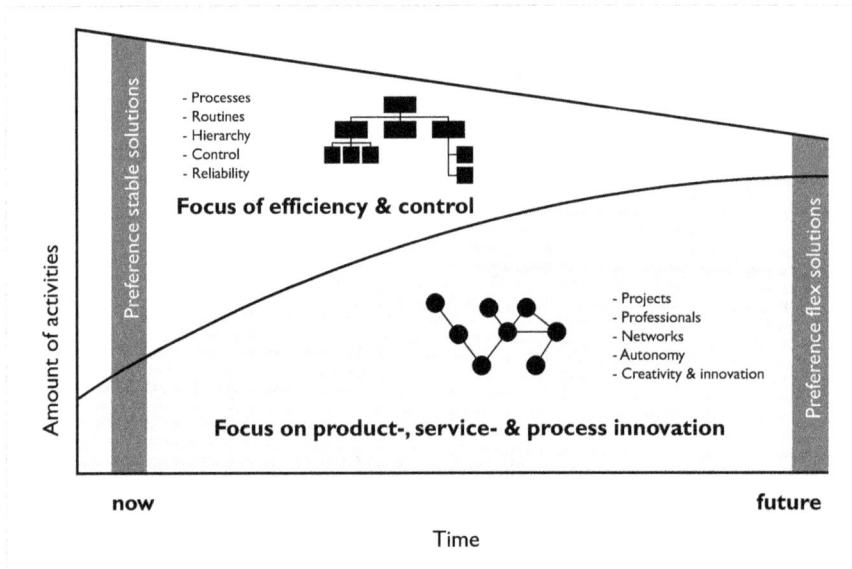

Figure 14. Expanding use of external sources

In the future the majority of persons contributing to a firm's success will actually not be employed by the firm in the classical sense (Figure 14). The firm will be an entity which expands and contracts continuously, whose composition is constantly changing and whose lifetime will be much shorter. Most firms will only have a small nucleus of people with a long term relationship with the firm. The team will remain the nexus of production, but the composition of teams will vary much more than in the past. Winning and competing are in most industries no longer only about developing an organization, but rather about finding the right resources for each individual project. In sport terms, winning and competing are no longer merely about coaching and developing a team for an entire season, but about selecting the right person for each individual game. At any particular moment, the coach is allowed to assemble the best team from all the different players available on the market to win the next game. Sometimes this requires better defense, sometimes improved offense. To attract the best and brightest for a particular assignment, the firm of the future will have to be able to manage its network.

We have seen that the traditional make-or-buy decision does not apply to knowledge work. The traditional make-or-buy decision will in the future only apply to routine, commodity type of products and services such as cloud computing (e.g. IAAS, PAAS, SAAS). In case of knowledge work, the make-or-buy decision is converted into a make-ally-or-buy decision where collaborations of various types will be the most dominant form. Employees are only hired to create, develop, apply, and retain very specific and tacit organizational knowledge. Complementary forms of knowledge will largely be obtained through partnerships while generic knowledge will be sourced through markets. Communities and crowds are particularly interesting as such new forms of collaboration are able to use the wisdom of large groups of people.[69] The boundaries of the firm will become wobblier and the firm will turn into a network in itself. The fuzzy firm will emerge. The fuzzy firm can perhaps best be compared to an octopus. Just like an octopus, the fuzzy firm can stretch itself very far (an octopus has four pairs of arms). It is very intelligent and flexible (allowing them to squeeze through tight places), and it has no or just a small core/skeleton. These characteristics make octopuses among the most intelligent and flexible creatures.

The fuzzy firm ≠ The flexible firm
More experienced academic scholars may observe that the concept of the fuzzy firm is somewhat related to the idea of the flexible firm. The idea of the flexible firm was started by John Atkinson in 1984 and got a lot of thought and a reasonable large following at the end of the last century.[70] The flexible firm aimed to give organizations the flexibility they needed in order to function in their ever changing environments. Flexibility was deemed important as the business environment became more complex, traditional industry boundaries were changing, and product life cycles were

---

69   James Surowiecki (2005). The Wisdom of Crowds. Anchor Books.
70   Henk Volberda (1998). Building the Flexible Firm, Oxford University Press

shortening. In those end-of-century days then corpulent corporations such as IBM and GM showed that even large multinationals needed to adjust to the environment in order to survive. So it was generally thought that more flexibility was really what was needed to cope with all these changes. However, in practice it is not easy to define flexibility properly. For instance, Homa Bahrami's colorful definition is: *'demanding agility and versatility; associated with change, innovation, and novelty; coupled with robustness and resilience, implying stability, sustainable advantage, and capabilities that evolve over time'.*[71] This definition is rather vague as concepts as versatility, agility are very much related. Around the same time, the end of the 20th century, various other related concepts of flexibility emerged. The most influential of these was the concept of dynamic capabilities, originally defined by David Teece and Gery Pisano as: *'The subset of the competences and capabilities that allow the firm to create new products and processes and respond to changing market circumstances'.* [72]

One of the key theories behind the flexible firm is the longstanding idea of Internal Labor Markets (ILM) by Peter Doeringer and Michael Piore. This theory basically suggests that the firm should make a long-term commitment to skillful workers by proving job security, structure, training, personal development, and career opportunities. Doeringer and Piore called these workers 'the primary sector' and argued that subcontracting and temporary work should be used to shield these valuable workers from the fluctuations in the economy.[73] This is the role of the secondary sector of the labor market. Perhaps the most persuasive application of the notion of a primary and secondary labor market is the core-periphery model. This model follows Doeringer and Piore and suggests that there are 'core' workers, who are a permanent part of the firm, are highly trained, and deeply committed to the firm. Then there are 'periphery' workers who preliminary provide flexibility, for instance against seasonal influences.

Although the core-periphery model has continuously been criticized in the academic literature, it has always had many followers, mainly in the real world but also among the academics. This large number of admirers can perhaps be explained by the fact that the notion of core 'worker' can easily be related to the familiar concept of core competence, a well-known element of strategic advantage in modern management literature.[74] Wherever modern management theory came up with the idea that core competences should be protected from substitution and imitation, HRM theorists and practitioners

71   Homa Bahrami (1992). The Emerging Flexible Organization: Perspectives from Silicon Valley, California Management Review, 33-52.
72   David Teece & Gary Pisano (1994). 'The dynamic capabilities of firms: An introduction. Industrial and Corporate Change, 3, 537-556.
73   Peter Doeringer & Michael Piore (1971). Internal Labor Markets and Manpower Analysis. Massachusetts. D.C. Heath and Company.
74   C.K. Prahalad & Gary Hamel (1990). The core competence of the corporation, Harvard Business Review, 79–91.

translated this notion of protecting core competences into protection of 'core' workers. The buzzword here became high-performance working practices (HPWP). Such practices are aimed at selecting, attracting, and promoting the best and brightest, paying them a good salary, and train, coach, and develop their skills. This should motivate these 'core'-workers to give their best and allow the firm to retain these core-workers. Naturally these HPW-practices were neither designed nor meant for the periphery worker. The role of the periphery workers in this core-periphery model is only twofold. First, to shield the core-worker from unpleasant economic fluctuations, and, second, to give the firm some numerical flexibility to adjust its productivity to demand without serious costs.

An interesting modification of this now classical core-periphery model is Charles Handy's 'Shamrock' organization. Charles Handy examined the future of work over twenty years ago. [75] He, being an Irishman, came up with the theory of the Shamrock organization, an organization with three leaves with a core of essential executives and employees. They are the heart of the business and possess knowledge, information, and networks that are crucial for the company. The core is supported by two other leaves. The second leave consists of external professionals in staff functions such as marketing, IT, and R&D. They are paid for their output, for well-defined products and services, not for their input. The third leave consists of the contract workers. These contract workers perform routine labor, are paid on output instead of input, and have mostly temporary and flexible contracts. Other writers have made a similar distinction as Handy.[76] For instance, James Brian Quinn distinguishes three types of activities in a company. First, the core activities, i.e. the activities the organization performs better than the competition. Second, the essential activities, i.e. the activities that are necessary in order to maintain the competitive advantage. These activities are complementary to the real core activities, but are nevertheless important. The third include all the peripheral activities. Quinn points out that the real core of a firm is usually minute. David Lepak and Scott Snell even distinguish four different groups of employees leading to a more applicable model.[77] Compared to the original core-periphery model, Lepak and Snell acknowledge that there is an important role for outside partners to provide unique, specific human capital. It also admits that there are some employees who have limited strategic values and whose capabilities are not crucial to the firm. This model acknowledges the fact that some periphery workers are much more valuable to the firm than some core employees.

---

75   Charles Handy (1989). The Age of Unreason, Business Books, London.
76   James Brian Quinn (1999). Strategic outsourcing, Sloan Management Review, 40, 23–26.
77   David Lepak & Scott Snell (1999). The human resource architecture: Toward a theory of human capital allocation and development, Academy of Management Review, 24, 31–48.

Criticism on the core-periphery model

As indicated, the core-periphery model and its modifications have been heavily criticized in the past.[78] First of all, the distinction between core and periphery workers is not so straightforward. It is therefore no surprise that related and later models of employment formulate a finer partitioning. We have seen that Quinn and Handy distinguish three different types of employment modes and Lepak and Snell even four. However, even with these four sets of employment modes it is very difficult to assign employees to a certain theoretical correct mode of employment. The core-periphery model oversimplifies the real world and its dynamics. In real life core and periphery workers often work closely together and sometimes even have the same job. Second, you cannot equate core competence with core worker. In many cases a core competence is a set of workers, augmented by organizational routines, a strong organizational identity and convincing brand name. There are extremely few individuals who are truly of unique strategic value. Moreover, these individuals are often very much aware of their special status and know how to attract these rents. Third, the idea that numerical flexibility needs to come primarily from the 'periphery' worker is rather silly. With fluctuations in the amount of work, core workers will also need to adjust to the total volume of work. The idea of numerical flexibility originates primarily from the manufacturing world where fluctuations are mainly seasonal. But with project firms in globalized markets the fluctuations are much larger, very much market driven, and involve important technological shifts. The loss or gain of one big project have often direct impacts on the amount of 'core' workers needed in a firm. During the periods of success, the firm needs to scale up very fast, and in the periods of decline they need to adjust fast as well. Fourth, the functional flexibility of professionals can reach only so far. It is not always efficient or even possible to teach employees new skills. In the age of hyper specialization, it might be better for both employee and firm to attract outside specialists to perform these new and different skills. Finally, the core-periphery model does not really specify what a peripheral worker actually means. Are we talking about alliances, partnerships, or temporary workers?

Overall the core-periphery is a flawed model. It argues that in the networked industries, such as the feature film or the music industry, the professionals who are actually doing the work (e.g. acting, performing, designing, creating) are the ones with the temporary contracts such as freelancers and contractors. The core of these firms seems to be flexible. It is the periphery, the supporting staff members, who have a longer term and stable employment relationship with the firm. This apparent inversion cannot be really explained by the traditional models of employment (Figure 15).

---

78   Arne Kalleberg (2001). Organizing Flexibility: The Flexible Firm in a New Century. British Journal of Industrial Relations, 39, 479–504.

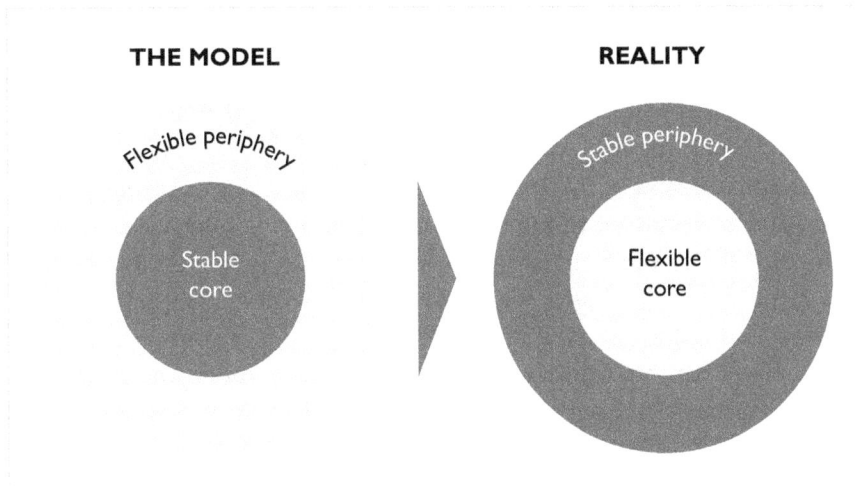

Figure 15. The inversion of the core-periphery model

The core-periphery model leads to organizations that expect their employees to become general managers. Organizations have constructed their whole career models on people moving up on the career ladder and thus supervising and leading an increasingly larger number of people. In most organizations there is a lack of career ladders for professionals and salary and bonuses are often capped if they do not want to become a general manager. This strategy may not always lead to the appropriate results as it undervalues specialists and overvalues (and invests) a large number of management skills.

Characteristics of fuzzy firms vs. flexible firms

The concept of the fuzzy firm resembles the concept of the flexible firm on a strategic level, as both concepts emphasize the importance of flexibility and continuous renewal, there are significant discrepancies. It is important to discuss these distinctions in detail to demonstrate the concept of the fuzzy firm more clearly. The first distinction is that the fuzzy firm is a knowledge-creating organization with an aim to solve complex problems in order to add value. The fuzzy firm needs flexibility to cope with the enormous fluctuations in highly competitive industries where individual knowledge and communities are the primary means of production. The fuzzy firm is not a manufacturing firm trying to cope with cyclical and seasonal fluctuations. This is crucial since the vast majority of research on the flexibility of firms have been done in traditional value chains such as manufacturing firms. Actual research on the fuzziness or boundarylessness of project based firms is limited. Second, where the flexible firm renews itself by training and development of its core employees, the fuzzy firm tries to connect to communities and knowledgeable outsiders and struggles to learn from them, for instance, by embracing them in hybrid projects. Third, the structure of the flexible firm is typically very hierarchical, although the high performance working practices may warrant some autonomy. In contrast to this, the structure of the fuzzy firm is very loose, or even nonexistent, outside the project at hand. In the flexible firm, there is a strong distinction between core and contingent workers. They are often physically separated and tend to perform different activities. In the fuzzy firm, outside professionals work hand in hand with long time insiders and it is often very hard to distinguish the employees from the contractors. Four, in the ideal flexible firm, the core worker has a relational contract with shared expectations of ideals and values as well as mutual respect and encouragement, the peripheral worker has a transactional contract where money is exchanged for performance.[79] In case of the fuzzy firm contracts are customized based on market standards. Sometimes these contracts are performance-based and of a short-term nature, in other instances these contracts are more relational. Five, in flexible firms, the career is largely determined by the organization; traditional career models such as Super's may still apply. In the fuzzy firm, the career is determined almost solely by the individual who looks for new assignments that add to the attractiveness of their portfolio of work. This assignment may be inside or outside the traditional organization; i.e. the firm. Six, a high level of trust between insiders is necessary in the flexible firms, while in the fuzzy firms an open culture is crucial. Outsiders and insiders constantly work together on the projects. All nodes of the network should have a feeling that they are valued and that they belong to the extended team. There is a high level of transparency and the simple rule is that professionals with the biggest amount of contribution should get the highest reward. Perceived unfairness will lead to disputes and will form obstacle for innovation and creativity. To avoid this, it is crucial that the firm explains the different roles in the network and clarifies the expectations and contribution of all parties as well as the resulting rewards.

The new functions of the future fuzzy firm

Bruce Kogut and Udo Zander have discussed the various functions of the firm: what do firms exactly do?[80] Based on their research the main functions of the firm are listed in Table 10,which also depicts in which respects the fuzzy firm is different from the traditional industrial firm. The first function of a firm is to be a legal entity that is able to give claims of profits to different parties. In the industrial era, the shareholders (i.e. the providers of capital) were entitled to the profits and the workers received a daily salary. In this system the shareholders take the risk of a non-performing firm. In the gig economy, there will still be a great need for the firm as a legal entity, but in a different way. First, the firm will be used more frequently as a

---

79 Denise Rousseau (1990).'New hire perceptions of their own and their employer's obligations: A study of psychological contracts', Journal of Organizational Behavior, I 38-94.
80 Bruce Kogut, & Udo Zander (1996). What firms do? Coordination, identity, and learning. Organization Science, 7, 502-518.

temporary legal vehicle, like in the feature film industry. These firms will dissolve within weeks, days or even hours of arrival. Second, a range of auxiliary legal contracts with different parties within the network will arrange the distribution of profits from additional resources and capabilities (e.g. intellectual property such as patents). Third, shareholders will not only be providers of capital, but also providers of networks, knowledge, and intellectual capital. It means that a larger and more varied group of shareholders have to be rewarded. Finally, capital providers will only be required to put up risky capital for the investment or to provide long-term guarantees to the clients. An important role of larger organizations will become that of a specialist insurance company, not so much different from the Lloyds of London. Although projects may be executed best by communities of independent specialists, large clients may still need some assurance and a point of contact when things go awry. Therefore, capital providers and insurance companies will sometimes need to guarantee the quality of projects by putting up capital. When a project does not deliver, these capitalist or insurance companies will cover losses. To mitigate the risks, these large risk providers will carry out projects audits, just as any insurance company will do.

Function	Industrial firm	Fuzzy firm
Organize distribution of cash flow & sharing of risks (legal)	Distribute property rights to providers of capital and labor	Distribute property rights to providers of knowledge and network. Capital is only needed for branding, product development, and managing risks
Limit self-interest behavior	Through the long term organizational career	Through reputation management and portfolio development
Provide sense of identity	A person's identity is largely based on the firm they work for	Identity shaped by profession, community, and firm
Promote knowledge development	Learning occurs within the context of the firm	Learning materializes in projects and within professional communities
Coordination of work	Coordination through hierarchies and in processes (HOW)	Coordination in projects (WHAT)

Table 6.   The changing role of the firm

The second role of the firm is to limit anti-social behavior. In the industrial era an employee spends his/her entire career for a single firm. Obviously having a long-term mutual relationship limits the tendency to self-interest. This remains a strong advocate for firms, but this role of limiting self-interest will slowly but surely taken over by internet, social networks, and communities. Reputation, portfolio, and resumes of individuals will increasingly be transparent.

The third role of the traditional firm is to be a powerful supplier of personal identity. In the new world, this will no longer be the case. Increasingly someone's profession will be the foremost supplier of identity, closely followed by community. Only in a number of cases the firm or sponsor will be a major source of belonging and identity.

The fourth role of the modern firm is to be a provider of knowledge development, innovation and learning. Increasingly this will and cannot occur within the boundaries of the firm. A huge amount of learning takes place in assignments across the boundaries of the firm and within professional communities where discourse and learning will come to pass between the specialists. Some of these communities will be virtual, while others will be much denser.

The fifth and final role of the firm is to deliver work coordination. This function of the firm is also rapidly changing. Where the industrial firm coordinates through hierarchies and processes, the coordination of fuzzy firms is much more subtle. Where coordination in the industrial era was a sine qua non, as otherwise goods cannot be produced, collaboration in the network economy is much more voluntary. In most cases a solo professional will be able to deliver value to clients, but through collaboration synergy effects will be unlocked. Obviously coordination does happen as a necessity within projects, but this will not always be provided by firms.

Capabilities and the virtuous cycle of fuzzy firms
Fuzzy firms strive to transform knowledge into income. To do so they need to develop three crucial capabilities: 1) acquiring attractive projects, 2) staffing the projects with appropriate resources, and 3) successful execution of these projects. Clearly, these three capabilities are not independent. When a firm acquires attractive projects, they can staff these assignments with professionals who are interested to get involved in these exciting projects. By attracting these skillful professionals, the chances of a successful execution of the project significantly increase. The successful execution of projects then enhances the possibility of getting new projects. Thereby the virtuous cycle of fuzzy firms is kick started.

The three capabilities of acquiring attractive projects, staffing them, and delivering proper results may differ in the characteristics of their building blocks (e.g. processes, people, structures). Depending on the type of deliverable, the variety and sort of knowledge that is shared and created, and the market a firm is operating within, the features of these capabilities may vary. For instance, some firms staff their projects primarily with internal employees, while other firms use their networks to find the right team in the crowd. Some fuzzy firms attract clients by great marketing and sales capabilities, others by means of reputation and branding. And finally, some fuzzy firms deliver results by offering unique, creative, and tailor-made solutions, others deliver results by delivering one-size fits all against minimal costs.

Case: The end of the resume

Earlier this year Oracle bought talent management service Taleo for $1.9 billion; the largest global database of talent resources. Thomas Kurian, Oracle's executive vice president for development, explained Oracle's motivations. *'We [..]want to create a talent directory. [It's] basically a portable talent profile that's attached to every employee or candidate, that's then integrated with recruiting and sourcing, so you can look outside of the company and look at all the pipelined candidates that are out there, and where you're considering sourcing from, to get a view of what the talent outside of the organization is. This allows you to find, recruit, and retain the best people.'* To do this, Taleo is building something called a talent profile; a digital portfolio that encapsulates your work history, set of skills, accomplishments, as well as your shortcomings. Ratings of your previous work (i.e. projects, assignments) will be an important part of these talent profiles. These talent profiles will become for individuals what reviews are for movies: essential. Their availability will not be limited to your current employer. A person's talent profile will be available in the cloud for anyone to see throughout the world. If you want to be considered for a job, you will have to participate. In the future firms will have the ability to scan the planet in real-time, gauging which person is best suited for a certain position. Whether these persons are currently inside or outside the org chart. Oracle's Taleo will not be without competition. Many large players (e.g. SAP, Salesforce. com) and small businesses (e.g. Truqu.com, GREX, Globoforce) are entering this field providing new and exciting solutions to the old-fashioned resume and traditional performance reviews.[*]

[*]   Source: http://blogs.hbr.org/cs/2012/06/crowdsource_your_performance_r.html

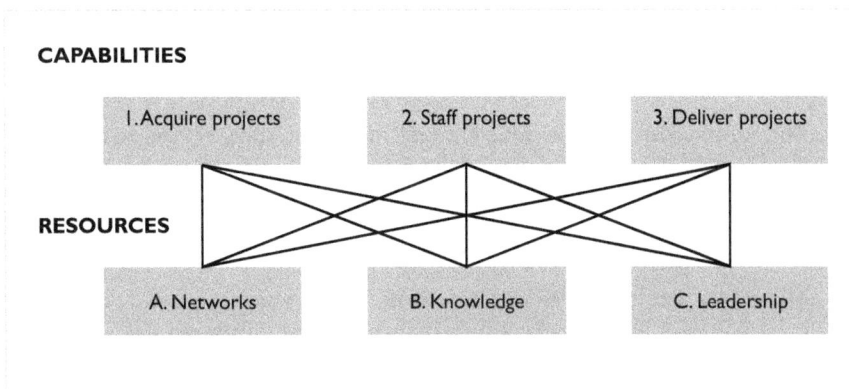

Figure 16. Capabilities and resources of fuzzy firms

In any case, the three key capabilities of the fuzzy firm (i.e. acquire projects, staff projects/find resources, and deliver projects) require, on a more abstract level, the same set of resources. To acquire a project, to staff it, and to deliver quality results, a fuzzy firm needs: a) knowledge, b) networks, and c) leadership skills (Figure 16). Using these three sets of resources, the capabilities of the fuzzy firm are able to locate opportunities and translate these opportunities into value added.

In the next chapters we will first discuss these three crucial resources (networks, knowledge, and leadership) in more detail. The careful reader may have noticed that capital, labor, and natural resources are not part of this set of resources. This is not because they are not important for the economy as a whole, but because these resources are, not crucial in the gig economy. After a brief discussion on these resources, the capability of staffing projects we will be discussed in more detail, which is probably one of the core aspects that sets the fuzzy firm apart from its 20th century equals.

Overview

1. Most firms consist of two parts: a diminishing portion of routine tasks, and a growing portion of knowledge work done in temporary projects.

2. Routine tasks can be outsourced or done in-house, depending on strategy and efficiency. Knowledge work typically requires collaboration with partners.

3. The amount of knowledge works is constantly expanding and contracting due to market factors and the time period of the projects. Firms can match this temporary nature of projects by offering temporary contracts. Market-type solutions such as communities, crowds, and market places become more attractive as a means of sourcing capabilities.

4. The boundaries of the firm are becoming wobblier and the firm becomes a network in itself. The fuzzy firm emerges. The trick is to manage networks and assemble teams.

5. The well-known core-periphery model does not apply to the real world and its assumptions are flawed. In the knowledge economy one cannot use a periphery to protect the core, but constant interaction between insiders and outsiders is needed to develop knowledge. This requires an open culture.

6. There is a virtuous cycle of fuzzy firms. When a firm acquires attractive projects, they can staff these assignments with professionals, thereby increasing the chances of a successful execution of the project. The successful execution then enhances the possibility of attracting new projects.

MANAGING THE FUZZY FIRM

CHAPTER 9:

CREATING KNOWLEDGE

66 The true sign of intelligence is not knowledge but imagination." Albert Einstein

In the industrial society we used to produce tangible goods. For each product, from bread to iron, there is a very concrete and physical production process that can be recorded in textbooks. But in the new network economy, the crucial factor of production is knowledge. Knowledge is shared, created, developed, and applied. However, in order to create knowledge, one should first possess some knowledge. In many cases specific professional knowledge is required to diagnose a situation properly and come up with the right solutions. Knowledge is therefore important since it is both an outcome and a necessary precondition for innovation. The increasing importance of knowledge can be witnessed in many areas. It is therefore no surprise that renowned researchers such as Raymond Miles and Charles Snow argue that the 21st century is the era of innovation. [81] Where until 1950 product specialization and standardization were the keys to competitive advantage and from 1950-2000 mass segmentation and marketing were the secrets of success, in the 21st century innovation is imperative (Figure 17).

Innovation can be defined as the translation of an idea or invention into something that adds value to people. An innovative idea is the one which is replicable at an economical cost and satisfies a specific need. To be

---

81   Raymond Miles, Charles Snow, John Matthews Grant Miles & Henry Coleman (1997), Organizing in the knowledge age; anticipating the cellular form, The Academy of Management Executive, 11, 7-24.

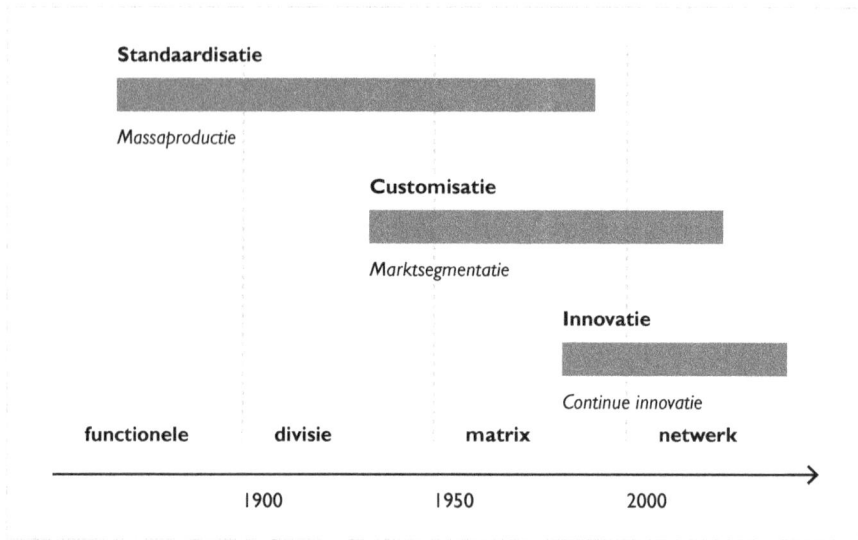

Figure 17. The innovation era has arrived

innovative one needs to combine knowledge, imagination, and initiative to obtain greater value from existing resources. An innovation can be either small or large and evolutionary or revolutionary. Most people think about product and service innovations, but process innovations (i.e. not changing the product per se, but the way the product is created) are almost just as important.

Creativity; the ticket to innovation

Creativity is the key driver of innovation. The difference between creativity is often the fact that some creative ideas are more useful than others. If these creative ideas have value for others they may be realized. So in short:

$$\text{Creativity} = \text{Ideas}$$
$$\text{Innovation} = \text{Ideas} + \text{Value} + \text{Realization}$$

Perhaps the most important theory describing the determinants of creativity is Teresa's Amabile's (1996) componential theory of creativity. This theory specifies that creativity requires a confluence of three components: [82]

1. **Domain-relevant skills.** These are Skills, Knowledge and Abilities (SKA's) in a particular domain. These skills are the basic building blocks upon which the individual can draw throughout the creative process.
2. **Creative skills.** These include a cognitive style and personality characteristics such as risk-taking, and taking new perspectives on problems, as well as discipline and skills in generating ideas.

---

82   Teresa M. Amabile (1996), Creativity in Context, Boulder, CO: Westview Press.

3. **Passion.** Intrinsic motivation to embark on a mission for the reason that it is exciting, encompassing, challenging, or enjoyable. Not because for other reasons such as monetary rewards or competition.

In the view of Amabile the environment can serve as an obstacle or as a stimulant to creativity through influencing motivation.

Producing and applying knowledge

Although our understanding of knowledge transfer and knowledge creation is still relatively limited, our understanding has increased significantly in recent years by the advances in scientific research. Knowledge transfer is the process through which one unit (e.g. individual, team, and organization) is affected by the experience of another. Although knowledge transfer is considered as important to organizational success, there is very little information about the underlying process through which knowledge transfer actually occurs. Recent studies show that the properties of knowledge are important for the knowledge transfer process. For instance, tacit knowledge is more difficult to transfer than explicit knowledge, knowledge that has not been codified is more difficult to transfer than codified knowledge, and knowledge that is not well-understood is also harder to transfer than the straightforward one. We also know that some factors facilitate the knowledge transfer process such as perceived status, level of trust, and frequency of interaction.[83]

Ikujiro Nonaka, Ryoko Toyama & Noboru Konno propose a model of knowledge creation with three building blocks: 1) knowledge assets, 2) the process of knowledge creation and 3) shared context. [84] To begin with, they argue that all knowledge-creation is based on available knowledge assets, which act as necessary inputs, outputs, and moderating factors of the knowledge-creating process. These assets are a necessary but not sufficient condition for value creation. As knowledge cannot be sold, due to problematic appropriability which we have discussed earlier, knowledge assets must be processed to realize their value. Nonaka, Toyama, and Konno put knowledge assets into four different categories: 1) experiential knowledge (i.e. the shared tacit knowledge within actors), 2) conceptual knowledge (i.e. explicit knowledge articulated through images, symbols and language), 3) systemic knowledge (i.e. packaged explicit knowledge), and 4) routine knowledge (i.e. tacit knowledge that is embedded in the actions and practices of the organization, such as: organizational culture and routines) (Figure 18). Secondly, they focus on the knowledge-creation

---

83   Bill McEvily, Vincenzo Perrone & Akbar Zaheer (2003), Trust as an Organizing Principle, Organization Science, 14, 91-103.
84   Ikujiro Nonaka, Ryoko Toyama & Noboru Konno (2000), SECI, Ba and Leadership: a Unified Model of Dynamic Knowledge Creation, Long Range Planning, 33, 5-34.

process. They argue that knowledge creation is a continuous process of dynamic interactions between tacit and explicit knowledge.[85] There are four basic forms of knowledge interaction:

1. **Socialization** (from tacit knowledge to tacit knowledge). The process of converting new tacit knowledge through shared experiences. A classic case of socialization is the traditional apprenticeship where apprentices learn the tacit knowledge needed in their craft through hands-on experience, rather than from written manuals or textbooks.
2. **Externalization** (from tacit knowledge to explicit knowledge). Externalization is the process of articulating tacit knowledge into explicit knowledge. Explicit procedures to increase quality are a typical example.
3. **Combination** (from explicit knowledge to explicit knowledge). Combination is the process of converting explicit knowledge into more complex explicit knowledge. Explicit knowledge is collected from various sources and then combined, edited, or processed to form new explicit knowledge. Using computers to combine and represent data in different forms is a well-known illustration of combining knowledge sets.
4. **Internalization** (from explicit knowledge to tacit knowledge). Internalization is closely related to 'learning by doing'. The classical example is reading a manual, before slowly but steadily improving the ability to operate a machine.

Thirdly, the authors argue that, besides knowledge assets and processes, the context is very important in knowledge-creation as such contexts provide the basis for individuals to interpret information to create meanings. They call this time-space context with physical, virtual, and mental subspaces Ba. Based on Japanese philosophy Ba is defined as the communal context in which knowledge is shared, created, and utilized. In knowledge creation, especially in socialization and externalization, it is important for participants to share context. Ba is the platform of knowledge creation by collecting the knowledge of the area into a certain time-space nexus. As Ba can be a mental or virtual place it does not have to be bound to a physical space. That the importance of context cannot be underestimated is also demonstrated by Mie Augier, Syed Shariq, and Morten Vendelø who indicate that to solve complex problems, one needs to create a shared context. Otherwise problem solvers cannot obtain verifications of similarities in understanding of knowledge and problems.[86]

85   Michael Polanyi (1958). Personal Knowledge. Towards a Post Critical Philosophy, London: Routledge.
86   Mie Augier, Syed Shariq & Morten Vendelø (2001). Understanding context: its emergence, transformation and role in tacit knowledge sharing. Journal of Knowledge Management, 5, 125 – 137.

Based on their vision of the knowledge-creating process and the three building blocks of knowledge creation, Nonaka et al. argue that the knowledge-creating process cannot be controlled, but leaders can facilitate knowledge creation by providing certain conditions. Leaders can provide the knowledge vision, facilitate the continuous spiral of knowledge interaction and create a shared context. Providing the knowledge vision gives direction to the knowledge-creating process by asking fundamental questions (i.e. what are we?, what should we create?, and where are we going?). Facilitating the dynamic process of building knowledge assets helps individuals create individual and collective knowledge. It should be noted that knowledge assets can hinder as well as foster knowledge creation. Organizations are subject to inertia and it is difficult for them to diverge from the course set by their previous experiences. Successful experience leads to excessive exploitation of the existing knowledge, and in turn hinders the exploration of new knowledge. The shared context can be built by providing physical space, such as meeting rooms, virtual space, such as a computer network, or mental space, such as common goals. To build context requires selecting the right mix of people and promote their interaction. For Nonaka et al. autonomy of the individual is very important. Not only does autonomy increase the commitment of individuals, but it is also a source of unexpected knowledge. By allowing individuals to act autonomously, an organization increases the chance of accessing and utilizing knowledge held by its members.

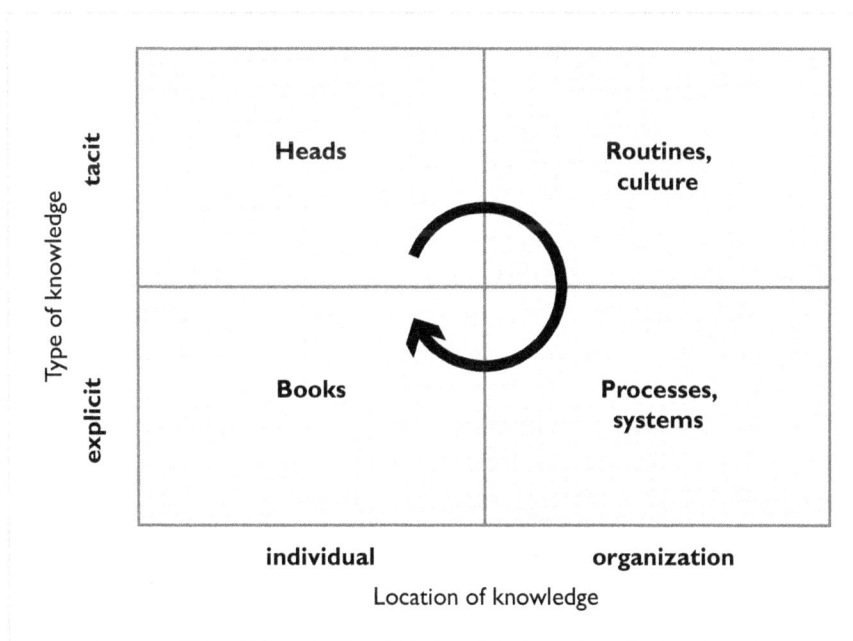

Figure 18. Areas where knowledge resides

Nonaka's model does not provide answer to a crucial question: To what extent is knowledge creation determined by the sheer genius of a single individual? Recent research, for instance, the study by Teppo Fellin and William Hesterly, seems to signal an increasing importance of the individual in knowledge creation process.[87] These and other studies seem to suggest that knowledge sharing and creation are largely determined by individual characteristics.[88] On the other hand, from Ikujiro Nonaka, Ryoko Toyama, and Noboru Konno we know that collective organizational elements such as trust and a shared context are essential for the production of knowledge.[89] Recent research conducted by Anita Woolley, Christopher Chabris, Alexander Pentland, Nada Hashmi, and Thomas Malone seems to support this point of view. Their research, where different groups had to accomplish a wide variety of projects, reveals that some groups perform well on almost every assignment, while other groups perform poorly on almost every assignment. Therefore they conclude that there is something like a collective intelligence. This collective intelligence does not depend on the average intelligence level of the group or on the intelligence of a single individual. There seems to be different factors that determine the collective intelligence of groups such as the social sensitivity of the team members and the proportion of women in the group. In short, this study suggests that having a group of smart people does not necessarily make the group smart.[90] This tells us that firms should not only focus on the selection of smart individuals, but also pay more attention to group performance. This may sometimes require changing the composition of groups and teaching groups better teamwork methods. Project teams should be selected and trained, not just individuals. Overall research on knowledge sharing and creation seems to point out that a combination of individual knowledge, the appropriate group composition, and a shared context and purpose are crucial for knowledge creation. Firms should select the right individuals to participate in groups responsible for knowledge creation and development. But it is a mistake to think that the core of valuable knowledge largely resides in knowledge repositories and organizational procedures. It resides in individuals and is stimulated and developed in collaboration efforts.

There are two significant trends that should be mentioned in any discussion on innovation. The first is the increasing value of open innovation efforts where individuals and organizations extensively collaborate across

87   Peter Drucker (1999). Management Challenges for the 21st Century, Butterworth-Heinemann, Oxford.
88   Teppo Felin & William Hesterly (2007). The Knowledge-Based View, Nested Heterogeneity, and New Value Creation: Philosophical Considerations on the Locus of Knowledge. Academy of Management Review, 32, 195-218.
89   Ikujiro Nonaka, R. Toyama & N. Konno (2000). SECI, Ba and Leadership: a Unified Model of Dynamic Knowledge Creation, Long Range Planning, 33, 5-34.
90   Anita Woolley, Christopher Chabris, Alexander Pentland, Nada Hashmi & Thomas Malone (2010). "Evidence for a Collective Intelligence Factor in the Performance of Human Groups", Science, 30 September.

organizational borders to come up with new ideas. The other trend is related and describes the involvement of users.

The succes of open innovation

Until recently most innovations were believed to come from of a relatively limited number of R&D labs. Only large companies such as Philips, Ericsson, and IBM could develop these massive R&D departments. Through innovation they could come up with new products and therefore enjoy large profits. These large industrial companies are increasingly in competition with young, small, flexible companies. It is striking that many of these young businesses have no major R&D departments, but use a completely other approach to pursue innovation; they work closely together with external firms to invent new products, services, and processes. As we speak many industries such as computers, telecommunications, chemistry, pharma, and biotechnology are transforming their innovation schemes.

Henry Chesbourgh was the first to argue that the future of innovation would be in collaboration across firm boundaries. In his own words: 'Open innovation is a paradigm that assumes that firms can and should use external ideas as well as internal ideas, and internal and external paths to market, as the firms look to advance their technology'.[91] The core of innovation does not reside within large central R&D facilities, but innovation is much more divided across many professional companies and universities. This trend towards open innovation has been particularly evident in the so-called high-tech industries, but also other sectors, such as banks, insurers, shop companies are now slowly moving in this direction. A good example of a FMCG company is Reckitt Benckiser. This company realizes many innovations with a relatively small innovation budget through collaboration with temporary and permanent partners. But even a colossal firm like P&G has adopted the open innovation approach and uses the slogan 'connect & develop' to show the importance of looking outward for R&D communities. Larry Huston and Nabil Sakkab show that open innovation is more than just a slogan at P&G.[92] They reveal that open innovation at P&G has led to an increase in successful product launches with 50% and an increase in R&D efficiency with 60%.

One of the key drivers of open innovation is the fact that innovation is progressively taking more place on the crossroads of external and internal knowledge. The innovation winners of tomorrow will be those organizations that are able to combine inside expertise with outside competences. This is

91 Henry Chesbrough (2003). Open Innovation: The New Imperative for Creating and Profiting from Technology, Harvard Business School Press, Boston, MA.
92 Larry Huston & Nabil Sakkab (2006). Connect and develop: Inside Procter & Gamble's new model for Innovation. Harvard Business Review, 84, 58-66.

not to say that open innovation is not with its drawbacks. Where the benefits of open innovation are obvious; a much larger pool of ideas, competences, and knowledge, the cost of open innovation are less apparent. But these collaboration costs can also be significant, from practical aspects such as intellectual property to structural aspects as the size, shape and nature of networks, and cultural aspects such as an open culture.

An active role for consumers

Eric von Hippel was one of the first scientists to show the important and active contribution of users in the innovation process. [93],[94] He argued that products are often created for a multitude of applications. Often the standard manner does not exactly correspond with the way the intended client wants to use it. This user therefore often customizes the product a little bit to make it fit. If producers use this knowledge of users properly to carry out improvements, a significant amount of value may be added to the products. For the UK Eric von Hippel, Jeroen de Jong, and Stephen Flowers[95] calculated that more than six percent of the population has adapted or created a consumer product. In total these 2.9 million people have invested over 179,000 person years in R&D (i.e. almost 100 hours per person per year). This R&D activity by users represents a value of roughly 2.3 billion pounds. This signifies that UK consumers invest 2.3 times more in R&D than all the UK companies together. It is therefore obvious that this source of innovation should be used more often and better. The additional observation that most major innovations come from users and not from organizations has also changed the process of innovation. Users are now much closer to the innovation process. BMW has recently set up a user community which is closely involved in the development of their sporting M-series. The rapid development of Firefox shows that user-communities can indeed be a very cost-effective method to innovate. This Web browser is developed by users under the coordination of the Mozilla Foundation. The browser can be downloaded for free, but business solutions are commercially developed based on patents of the Mozilla Platform MozDev Group.

That there is a significant role for users in innovation has been vigorously demonstrated. But perhaps even these studies underestimate the real magnitude of open innovation and user involvement. Most of the current studies have been done in manufacturing firms and R&D institutes. But, as we have seen, our economy is nowadays largely a service economy, even in the manufacturing sector. This is a world where value is not objectively determined, but is co-created. The customer experience is vital

93   Eric von Hippel (1986). Lead users: a source of novel product concepts, Management Science, 791–805.
94   Eric von Hippel (1988). The Sources of Innovation, Oxford University Press PDF.
95   Eric von Hippel, Jeroen de Jong & Stephen Flowers (2010). Comparing business and household sector innovation in consumer products: Findings from a representative survey in the UK. MIT Sloan School of Management, Working Paper.

to value creation. Tangible products are often not more than a means to an end. Nowadays this transition is perhaps best evident in the world of IT where 'the cloud' is possibly the buzzword of today's economy. Tangible products such as hardware, platforms, and software are transformed into services. In this world open innovation and user involvement are even more important to value creation[96]. Perhaps the importance of co-creation is best seen in the new upcoming field of service design[97] where people, platforms, participation, co-creation and design are crucial elements used to innovate and enhance the value of services.

A framework for innovation capabilities

It is clear from the above that cross-border collaboration with users and other outside individuals is an important trend that has great potential for innovation. The success of open innovation and user involvement has given firms more awareness regarding the possibility to organize their knowledge both internally and externally. It is not always beneficial for firms to keep their knowledge for themselves. True value added knowledge production requires cross-borders collaboration. This is true for all three aspects of knowledge production: knowledge exploration, knowledge retention, and knowledge exploitation. First, a firm can create knowledge or buy it on the market. Second, to retain this knowledge, firms can incorporate this knowledge within the firm, or within the network of the firm (i.e. partners, alliances). Third, in applying or exploiting knowledge, firms are confronted with the 'keep-or-sell' problem. By combining these aspects of knowledge creation with the borders of the firm a framework emerges which describes six different organizational capabilities required in an innovative organization.[98] (Figure 19)

The six capabilities of an innovative firm are:

1. **Inventive capability.** This refers to a firm's ability to generate new knowledge internally. Inventive capacity is largely determined by the level of existing knowledge in a specific area within a firm because existing knowledge facilitates the generation and integration of new knowledge.
2. **Absorptive capability.** This relates to exploring external knowledge. This may entail the acquisition of outside knowledge or learning from outside knowledge and bringing it into the firm.

96   Henry Chesbrough (2011). Open Services Innovation: Rethinking Your Business to Grow and Compete in a New Era.
97   Marc Stickdorn & Jakob Schneider (Eds.) (2011). This is Service Design Thinking: Basics - Tools – Cases.
98   Ulrich Lichtenthaler & Eckhard Lichtenthaler (2009). A Capability-Based Framework for Open Innovation: Complementing Absorptive Capacity. Journal of Management Studies, 46, 1315-1338.

3. **Transformative capability.** This represents the capability of a firm retaining knowledge in procedures, routines, culture, and employees internally.
4. **Connective capability.** This relates to the capability of a firm of retaining knowledge within its network. These external networks have to be maintained and managed over time, which implies that information and knowledge has to be shared and, unlike absorptive capability, connective capability is a two-way street where partners share knowledge.
5. **Innovative capability.** Here ideas and inventions are transformed into innovations that resonate with the market and clients. These ideas and inventions may be developed internally or acquired from external sources
6. **Desorptive capability.** This describes a firm's capability to apply their knowledge on behalf of other firms that may be better positioned to fully exploit the advantages of an invention.

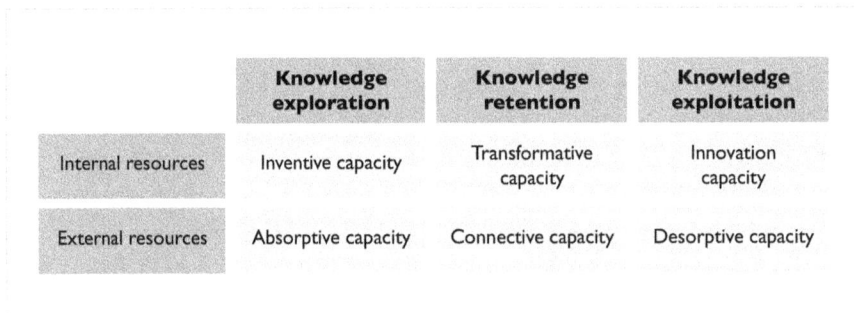

	Knowledge exploration	Knowledge retention	Knowledge exploitation
Internal resources	Inventive capacity	Transformative capacity	Innovation capacity
External resources	Absorptive capacity	Connective capacity	Desorptive capacity

Figure 19. Different organizational capabilities support innovation

The framework of Ulrich Lichtenthaler and Eckhard Lichtenthaler tells us that an organization needs different capabilities to ensure the productive use of knowledge. These capabilities have different elements on various levels (individual and organizational). They argue that there is no such thing as make-or-buy, but that a firm has to balance different knowledge capacities at the same time. Obtaining and developing knowledge inside and outside the organization.

Overview

1. Amabile's model shows that creativity is determined by motivation, domain specific skills and creative skills.

2. Nonaka's theory teaches us that in order to create knowledge, a firm has to invest in trust and establish a shared context.

3. Innovation, whether it is innovation of processes, products, and services, is not something that can be done in-house, but often requires collaboration with partners.

4. In the service economy, there is an important role for users to cocreate and co-innovate.

5. In order to build this 'innovation capability' firms need different capacities. Some of these capacities are internal to the firm, other are related to the networks of firms.

CHAPTER 10:

MANAGING NETWORKS

66 Everything and everyone what does not have value, according to what is valued in networks, or ceased to have value, is switched off the networks and ultimately discarded " Manuel Castells, The Rise Of The Network Society, 1996, p. 134

The old mantra of Alfred D. Chandler; 'structure follows strategy', will still hold true in the information economy.[99] But where Mr. Chandler originally thought about M-structures versus F-structures and other sorts of organizational hierarchies, in the information economy we are looking for the best network structures to ensure the creation and application of knowledge. The newest organizational designs are therefore no longer M-forms, matrix organizations or multi-firm networks. The new organizational designs, such as the I-form organization, reflect the reality of cross border collaboration between individuals in networks.[100] Until very recently, networks were rather abstract concepts, but nowadays they are very concrete and tangible entities which can be made visible on any computer device including mobile phones. Nevertheless, there are quite some discussions on the precise definition of a network. This study makes therefore a distinction between networks, communities, and crowds (Figure 20).

99 Alfred Chandler (1962). Strategy and Structure: Chapters in the History of the American Industrial Enterprise. Cambridge, MA: MIT Press.
100 Raymond E. Miles, Grant Miles, Charles C. Snow, Kirsimarja Blomqvist & Hector Rocha (2009). The I-Form Organization, California Management Review, 54, 61-76.

Networks, communities & crowds

The community of a firm consists of everyone who works for the organization as well as all the direct contacts of the firm. The direct contacts can be customers, users or suppliers. In any case, there is often a long-standing relationship between the firm and these members. The network of the firm consists of the contacts of the community; the links between the employees, customers, and suppliers. These people are important because they can offer opportunities. Outside the firm's network is the crowd with whom no cordial, long-term relationship can be established.

A community is a group of people around a common goal. In a community, there is a lot of mutual communication and members feel connected to each other. Sometimes a very active role is required from the members, but often the desired input of members is limited and is on voluntary basis. Depending on the community, there are either formal rules or only informal standards. There may be a clear hierarchy with clear leaders, but there can also be a much decentralized decision-making structure. In short, there is a great diversity in communities. Unlike a community, a crowd has no common purpose. Everyone in a crowd pursues their own individual goals. There is also no long-term goal between the firm and the crowd. Collaborations are short and last as long as needed.

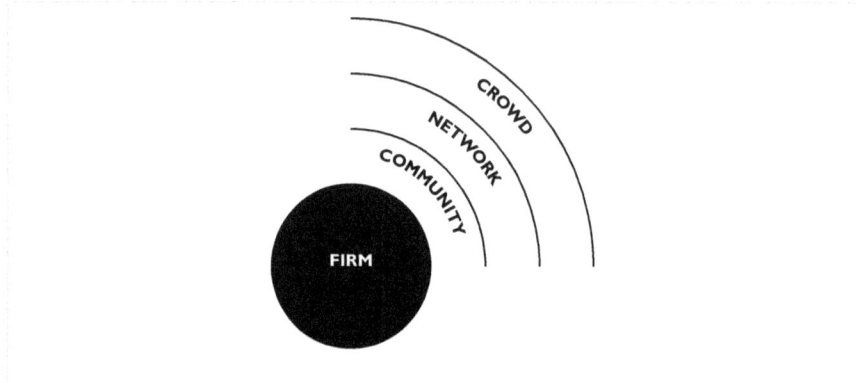

Figure 20. Communities, networks & crowds

Communities can be catagorized according to their target audience. There are internal, external, and hybrid communities (Figure 21):

1. Internal communities of employees are numerous. Every large organization has at least one community. These firms often put a lot of energy and money in the creation and maintenance of these communities. The aim is to foster internal collaboration and communication.
2. External communities give limited insight into the internal processes of an organization. Their understanding of the organization is often based

on the image of the organization. The goal of such communities is often to connect external parties such as clients to the firm.

3. In hybrid communities external participants and contributors are given more understanding of the organization. There are two main types of hybrid communities: supplier communities and user communities:
   a. Supplier communities contain participants of the organization and its suppliers. The number of the suppliers of these communities can vary from a few to thousands of different vendors. Examples are Wal-Mart and IKEA.
   b. User communities consist of an organization and the main users of a particular product or service. These are often users who use the product or service intensively and have an impact on the development of the product or service.

Thomas Malone, Robert Laubacher, and Chrysanthos Dellarocas have developed a method to identify and understand the differences between crowds, networks, and communities more systematically. They show that there are many subtypes of communities, networks and crowds. These communities, networks, and crowds differ in their a) decision making system, b) nature of existence, and c) teamwork method. Based on their research, Malone, Laubacher, and Dellarocas conclude that crowds work best when the activities can be executed independently. Communities work best if cooperation is needed to solve a problem since mutual trust and a shared context are crucial.

While crowdsourcing is a relatively new concept, there has already been some research on the quality of the ideas derived from crowds.[101] Researchers like Barry Bayus and Marion Poetz and Martin Schreier compared the ideas of crowds with ideas of internal professionals.[102] They concluded that the ideas

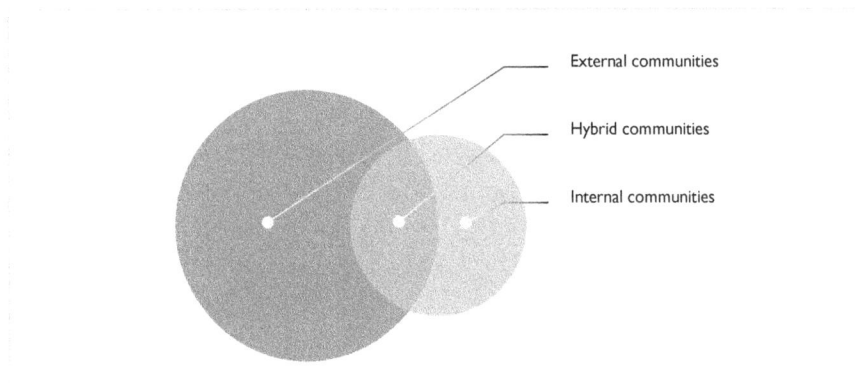

External communities

Hybrid communities

Internal communities

Figure 21. Internal and external communities

101 Barry Bayus (2010). Crowdsourcing and individual creativity over time:the detrimental effects of past success, Working paper Kenan-Flagler Business School, University of North Carolina.
102 Marion Poetz & Martin Schreier (2012).The Value of Crowdsourcing: Can Users Really Compete with Professionals in Generating New Product Ideas?. Journal of Product Innovation Management, 29, 245–256.

of crowds score higher on renewal and customer benefits than the ideas of internal professionals, but the ideas of crowds score somewhat lower on their application possibilities. Poetz and Schreier therefore conclude that the ideas of crowds are complementary to the traditional process of innovation within companies.

Advantages and disadvantages of open and closed networks

Networks are very instrumental to modern organizations. Networks determine what you see as your opportunities and threats, and also whether you are able to grab those opportunities. However, it is not easy to determine what the optimal network of an organization looks like. Should you run a big or small organizational network? Should it be directed inward or outward? Does an optimal network revitalizes itself quickly or is it pretty stable? Do all the people in a network need to know each other (i.e. dense) or should there be a lot of loose connections? These are important questions because each type of network characteristic determines the effectiveness of your knowledge creation, development, and application.

Traditionally, people have always had a rather limited number of social relationships which were, for the most part, quite stable. It is difficult to exactly calculate the maximum number of social relationships a person may have, but the much-quoted number of Dunbar states that a person can manage personal relations with approximately 150 individuals. However, with the rise of social media it is now possible to have a 'personal' relationship with many more people. On the internet someone may have more than 1000 Facebook friends, 1500 Linked In contacts, and 10,000 followers on Twitter. So through the rise of social media, individuals are able to manage and frequently contact a much larger personal network. Social media enables us to keep in touch with far-off friends, disparate colleagues, and remote strangers. This is important because we know that these so-called weaker ties are often much more useful to us since they open bridges to new worlds with new knowledge and opportunities. [103] This in contrast with strong ties (i.e. family, friends, and close colleagues) who tend to give us more information about worlds we already know enough. Weak ties are better when it comes to finding new assignments, ideas, experts, and knowledge. With social media it has become much easier to manage these weak relationships and to use their knowledge and network.

Gary Pisano and Robert Verganti rely on social network theories which enable them to determine the ideal network structure of a firm.[104] To understand their arguments it is very important to understand that every

103 Mark Granovetter (1973). "The Strength of Weak Ties". The American Journal of Sociology, 78, 1360–1380.
104 Gary Pisano & Robert Verganti (2008). Which Kind of Collaboration Is Right for You? Harvard Business Review, December 2008.

The Fuzzy Firm™

firm is essentially a network in itself which resides and operates in a much larger network. A traditional hierarchical company has the typical characteristics of a network with strong inner connections and a handful of weak outer connections. In contrast, an open-source community such as apache.org, has many members with weaker inner connections.

	Closed networks	Open networks
Advantages	• Shared context and potentially high trust • Limited risks and costs • Teams tend to be productive quickly • Knowledge is retained by high loyalty and strong group identity	• Large and diverse set of resources • High productivity through deployment of experts • More solutions and more creative solutions • Greater competition
Disadvantages	• Limited number of available resources • High training costs • Low renewal rates • Groupthink, tunnel vision • Limited creativity/innovation • Tendency toward self-gratification	• Great diversity in knowledge and context • Higher costs and greater risks • As a general rule, require more time to be productive • More chances of knowledge loss by low loyalty and retention

Table 7.   Advantages and disadvantages of open and closed networks

A dense and closed network, such as the traditional firm, has a number of important benefits. First, the members of a closed network function in a similar and shared context. They typically have a shared understanding of reality, and possibly, a high level of mutual trust. These aspects can be a great advantage. Think about the US Marines who have to trust each other to perform a difficult task. They have to know and understand each other as well as one's capabilities and weaknesses. But such strong links are similarly important for a firm that operates in a very specific niche. As there are not many people who understand this knowledge and appreciate the social context, there tend to be strong links between the people working in such a small and dedicated field of expertise. Second, the cost of maintaining a closed network (i.e. searching, selecting, and accepting partners) is relatively low and the associated risks are much smaller. Third, a team assembled from a closed network is often much quicker in production mode because not much time is wasted by storming and norming.[105] Fourth, there is little loss of knowledge in close networks because people often remain a member of the group for a long time by their great loyalty and shared identity.

Of course, closed networks have their own disadvantages too. First, the chance that the required knowledge is actually present and available

---

105   Bruce Tuckman (1965). Developmental sequence in small groups. Psychological Bulletin, 63, 384–99.

within a closed network is much smaller. This is particularly true when the necessary knowledge or competences is not part of the core of the firm. Second, a closed network loses a lot of time, energy, and productivity by developing new knowledge. Third, the creativity of closed networks may be limited due to the restricted number of innovative ideas and viewpoints. This lack of creativity in small networks may be aggravated by the greater chance of tunnel vision and groupthink. New opinions are more difficult to express in closed networks with their strong cultures. This is the way we do things around here, is an often heard catchphrase in closed networks. Finally, individuals in closed networks tend to develop an unrealistic image of the outside world.

The Impact of Web 2.0

World Wide Web inventor Tim Berners-Lee envisioned the Web to be *'a collaborative medium, a place where we [could] all meet and read and write'*.[106] This early vision became reality around the millennium with the arrival of Web 2.0 functionality. With Web 2.0 we hereby mean those web features that facilitate information sharing and collaboration on the internet. Users interact and collaborate with each other. They are both creators and consumers in a virtual community which they themselves cocreate. Although virtually everyone uses web 2.0 functionality, there is no comprehensible definition of the concept. Andreas Kaplan and Michael Haenlein[107] distinguish six different types of web 2.0 functionality based on a dichotomy between media richness (i.e. the amount of information per unit time) and ego presentation (i.e. the extent to which the presentation of the ego is important). The resulting six types are:

1. **Collaboration.** Websites aimed at mass collaboration can lead to better, more creative, and more efficient outcomes than traditional alliances and partnerships in real-life between a limited number of people. undoubtedly Wikipedia is currently the best known collaboration website.
2. **Blogs.** Blogs are often created by a single person, but there are also teams who blog together and as such threaten the traditional media. Perhaps the best example here is the Huffington Post.
3. **Content communities.** The idea behind these websites is to share and make available content to the community. *Content communities* exist for all types of media such as presentations (SlideShare), videos (YouTube), books (BookCrossing), and photos (Flickr).
4. **Social networking sites.** These websites enable networking with people and share messages and other stuff within the network. The most well-

106 http://news.bbc.co.uk/2/hi/technology/4132752.stm
107 Andreas Kaplan & Michael Haenlein (2010). Users of the world, unite! The challenges and opportunities of social media, Business horizons, 53, 59-68.

known social networking sites are probably Facebook and Linked In, but there is a large variety in special purpose networks.

5. **Virtual games.** Think about games like *'World of Warcraft'* which often provide a 3D environment.
6. **Virtual worlds.** These are virtually identical to virtual games, but give the user more personal branding possibilities (e.g. *'Second Life'*).

		Media richness		
		Low	Average	High
Ego presentation	High	Blogs	Social network sites (Facebook)	Virtual worlds (Linden, Second Life)
	Low	Collaboration (e.g. Wikipedia)	Content communities (You Tube)	Virtual games (World of Warcraft)

Table 8.   Web 2.0 functionality

It is certainly true that web 2.0 has already had a huge impact on the economy. Within a couple of years Facebook and Twitter will become important channels for companies in their dealings with customers and recruiting new employees. But web 2.0 tools have not yet lived up to its full potential. If web 2.0 really succeeds in establishing new forms of collaboration, it will have a gigantic influence on work as we know it. First, as said through social networking, one can build and maintain strong relationships with a much larger group of individuals. We will not only collaborate with colleagues, but increasingly with customers, suppliers, and many other stakeholders on the same platform. Second, with the rise of new collaboration tools like *SharePoint, Dropbox* and *Google docs* the cost of cross border cooperation are rapidly diminishing. It is now possible to work together intensively with a variety of partners at the same time for almost no cost. Now businesses can mobilize the collective intelligence of large groups and this collective intelligence often leads to much better outcomes in terms of quality and efficiency. This continuous drop in transaction costs facilitates cross border working even further.

The potential impact on the way we work can be seen from the huge public attention towards initiatives like The Future of Work and Work 2.0.[108] It is clear that new technologies are making it possible to cooperate and collaborate with much larger groups, giving customers more proactive roles, and lead to vanishing boundaries between the firm, suppliers, and clients. Moreover, technological progress enables organizations to use the wisdom of crowds and the collective intelligence to be more innovative and offer better services. Having said that, it still may take a lot of time and

---

108 http://thefutureofwork.net/

energy before the full potential of these technologies is actually realized; new network structures need to emerge and managers and employees need to adjust to new ways of working.

Creating collaborative business communities

There has been a growing interest in communities with the advent of new social technologies and the increased importance of collaboration, creativity, and diversity. There seems to be real, tangible positive effects of these collaborative communities. Several businesses which have already started with these communities such as Sungard report higher margins on knowledge work as a result of the creation of these collaborative communities.

Naturally there are various types of communities. Just as the structure of an organization follows its strategy, the community characteristics are a result of the community objectives. These goals should be clear to all involved. Is the community aimed at knowledge sharing (communities of practice) or is there more at stake? Does the community, for instance, report vacancies? Is the community open to outsiders? Communities vary in the following aspects:

1. **Size.** Some communities are quite small while others are many times larger than the business itself. Especially knowledge networks tend to become large platforms where professional share information which are much larger than most businesses.
2. **Scope.** The most common distinction between communities is between internal, external, and hybrid communities. Who can apply for membership? Is it a community for suppliers or a hybrid community where employees and contractors are mixed?
3. **Relevance.** The relevance of the network has to do with width of the available services on the community. Is this merely knowledge-sharing and communication or is knowledge created and applied as in Joomla and Mozilla communities?
4. **Contract.** What is the nature of the relationship between the community and its members? What do members bring and what does the community does in return?
5. **Renewal.** How do you ensure that membership renews itself and the community does not become too protected and closed for renewal? Is there an entry fee, or are there certain conditions for entry?
6. **Platform.** Is the community supported by knowledge and collaboration tools? What is the ideal combination between online and offline activities?
7. **Leadership.** How is the community co-created and co-led?

Currently, any professional knowledge organization needs various communities for people to share and create knowledge. The question is what kinds of communities does an organization need? And what does this mean for the organization itself and its employees? In theory, communities have a number of potential advantages:

1. The cost of knowledge is flexible (Knowledge-as-a-service: KAAS)
2. The process of selection and onboarding is more effective, efficient, and faster;
3. Knowledge is not lost to the competition but retained;
4. Communities may attract individuals who are not interested in a long-term relationship;
5. A community fosters a sense of belonging leading to a culture of contribution.

Moreover, as more and more knowledge domains will be supported by specialized platforms and communities, it is likely that there will be increasing competition between platforms in the future. By creating your own hybrid platforms, the organization may attract new business and new, scarce resources. It is important to understand the meaning of co-creationship. For a community to thrive, the community manager has to strike a fine balance between leading and listening. The growth of a community should be somewhat organic and a culture should be molded not dictated.

The rise of social network analysis
Regrettably, virtual social networks such as Linked In are still being used as a kind of glorified card catalog, while the potential value of these social networks is much larger. One of the techniques to measure and visualize this potential value is by means of social network analysis (SNA). SNA has the power to open the *'black-box'* of the informal organization. Lately SNA has become increasingly important as it reveals who knows whom both inside and outside the organization. Network analyses is a new mode of analyzing the structure and the information flows inside and outside the organizations. Which departments communicate with each other? Who are the actual informal leaders? How big is the network of the organization and how is the organization connected to the network around it? Does the network of the organization refreshes itself rapidly or is there a fairly consistent network with the same individuals on new positions? Just as networks, social network analyses are not new at all. Family and friends networks have been analyzed for decades and in the late 80s various business networks were already studied. But there is a striking and big difference between the long-established analyses of business networks and the current possibilities. Up to about five years ago, SNA was often performed at the organizational

level; alliances and other partnerships between companies were visualized and analyzed. Nowadays social network analyses are typically performed on the level of the individual using large datasets. To create these analyses, collected data from the mobile phones, email and social networking sites are used to determine the flow of information. This leads to a better understanding of shared information and the real underlying structure of the firm and the network in which it operates. This type of analyses will also show the added value of partners. Do new partners open bridges to new networks and areas of knowledge? Or do they connect to the same sources of information and individuals as the current partners? You can also track developments of your network over time.

Coworking communities
Networking has substantial costs. This is something that is quite often forgotten in network analysis. Although the transaction costs of networking have decreased dramatically through the introduction of social media, as even Dunbar's number of 150 personal relations seems somewhat outdated now, twittering, linking, posting, and meeting people face-to-face will always be time consuming. As every individual has limited time and networking does not bring in cash directly, people tend to pick out those communities with the highest expected benefit and a limited investment of time and money. Therefore, today's buzzword is 'relevance'. Relevant networks are those that offer a range of benefits that are applicable to an organization or individual needs.

There are a lot of examples of networks that offer multiple benefits to individuals. Harvard Business School does not only provide a great education but, perhaps more importantly, a great and valuable life-time network. A special case of such relevant networks is the traditional firm. A good firm is able to assist individuals with obtaining knowledge, meeting the right people, and finding suitable assignments.

Coworking spaces are a more recent and emerging example of relevant networks. Coworking is a working style which involves a shared working environment. This could be an office, a bar, or a restaurant. Coworking spaces are open to all sorts of professionals and you do not have to be affiliated with a specific firm. These coworking spaces are especially attractive to independent professionals, but they also attract employees from small and big firms that are able to work efficiently away from the office using internet and collaboration tools.

Coworking spaces were originally started by solo entrepreneurs seeking an alternative to working in coffee shops and work from home. These entrepreneurs needed a place that facilitated their need for social contacts, a sense of belonging, and possibilities for cooperation and collaboration. Although some people just needed a place to work quietly, away from the noise at home and in the restaurants and bars they used to visit. Many coworking spaces try to turn themselves into something more than just a space. They want to become a community; a group of people who share the same values. Sometimes these coworking communities go even further and share networks, knowledge, and other services than just accommodation. These coworking communities tend to be very informal, but as the number of links and shared services grows, the need for formalization is also expanding.

Case: The Hub

An interesting example of a company where a shared higher purpose is important is the *coworking* organization, The Hub. The Hub provides small entrepreneurs workspace in so-called, Open Flex Offices. What distinguishes The Hub from other Flex offices is their explicit pursue of a higher goal. In the words of The Hub: 'we're a social enterprise with the ambition to inspire and support imaginative and enterprising initiatives for a better world. The Hub is a global community of people from every profession, background and culture working at 'new frontiers ' to tackle the world's most pressing social, cultural and environmental challenges. ' By explicitly pursuing a greater purpose ('social innovation') the 4,000 small entrepreneurs who work at one of the 30 Flex offices of *The Hub* feel more connected. This closeness will create more cooperation between enterprises, not only at office level, but also virtually.

Not all coworking communities are successful. In general there are four requirements for launching any coworking community. First of all, the quality of the host plays an essential role. Someone needs to be the center of the hub, a person who is able to connect different people and can make sure that all the essential elements, i.e. all the hygiene factors, of the accommodation are taken care of. Second, all the participants need share the same goal or vision. Such an aspiration can unite people. If the workers pursue unrelated or even contrasting goals, it will be hard to connect these people and to offer more than just a workplace. If some of the members of the coworking space would like to work quietly while others look for collaboration possibilities, the chances for success are slim. Third, a certain physical space is needed to promote collaboration and communities. Anne-Laure Fayard and John Weeks argue than any office-space needs to strike a fine balance between proximity, privacy, and permission in order to foster cooperation. [109] Fourth, in an ideal situation the coworking space has members which possess capabilities that resemble each other to a certain extent, but which are not

---

109   Anne-Laure Fayard & John Weeks (2011). Who Moved My Cube?, Harvard Business Review, July.

completely identical. There is related variety. This helps members to find synergies within the community. However, this quality is not required for a successful coworking space, but it is important if the coworking community wants to add value beyond a social context.

These relevant coworking communities may in fact be a future model for the modern firm. In these communities, there is a need for a modern type of manager, an individual who makes sure that all the basics needs are taken care of and different people are connected. Just as a modern firm, there needs to be synergy between the people. There needs to be a vision, shared ideals and a strategy towards selecting community members. Finally, also like a modern firm, there is a substantial amount of professional autonomy for the workers who all have to bring in their expertise to win new assignments in ever changing groups.

Overview

1. Networks are one of the crucial production factors of tomorrow's economy. Networks come in different shapes and forms, but can be distinguished from the firm itself, and a firm's communities and crowds.

2. The optimal structure of the network essentially depends on knowledge that is created and the value that is added. Sometimes open networks are better, for other production processes closed networks function better.

3. The arrival of social media has given tremendous possibilities to firms to overcome the traditional barriers of coordination and collaboration. These new tools enable professionals to collaborate across borders and time zones.

4. Networking is time consuming. Even though the arrival of internet has made it possible for individuals to maintain large networks, the size of the network is constrained by time and energy. Network relevance is crucial; maintaining relationships with those network contacts that are relevant for you and your business such as knowledge providers, clients, staffing agencies, and talent coaches. These are most likely people who resemble you, but are different from you (related variety).

CHAPTER 11:

LEADING PROFESSIONALS

" The most important, and indeed the truly unique, contribution of management in the 20th century was the fifty-fold increase in the productivity of the manual worker in manufacturing. The most important contribution management needs to make in the 21st century is similarly to increase the productivity of knowledge workers." Peter F. Drucker[110]

According to the Webster dictionary, a professional is someone who is engaged in a calling, requiring specialized knowledge, and often long and intensive preparation. David Maister, probably the most eminent business thinker on professionals and professional firms, lists four elements that characterize all professionals.[111] First, exercising a profession requires highly valued specialist knowledge, abilities, and skills. Second, professionals have a large autonomy in exercising their profession. Third, originality and creativity are important in exercising the profession, and, fourth, professionals have a strong professional identification (e.g. profession standards).

As was mentioned earlier, in his classic article on knowledge-worker productivity, Peter Drucker states that we humans were able to increase the production of manual labor fiftyfold in the 20th century. But Peter Drucker furthermore asserts that this task has been relatively easy and

---

110 Peter Drucker (1991). The New Productivity Challenge. Harvard Business Review, Nov-Dec.
111 David Maister (1993). Managing the Professional Service Firm, Free Press, New York.

straightforward. The task for our current 21st century, to increase the productivity of knowledge work and knowledge workers, is much and much more difficult. According to Peter Drucker there are six factors that are crucial in advancing the productivity of professionals.

1. The task of professionals needs to be clearly defined. Only when there is a clear and unambiguous assignment, the productivity of the professional can be improved.
2. Professionals have to have complete autonomy. They are responsible for managing themselves.
3. Professionals will have to face the responsibility for permanent innovation.
4. Professionals need to learn continuously from each other and from the experiences on the job.
5. Sponsors and professionals should look at quality of deliverables not at the quantity. The quality of output is more important than the quantity of output.
6. Professionals need to be seen and treated as an 'asset' rather than a 'cost'.

Even though we have had these six basic ingredients for some time, we, as a society, have not been very good in bringing these elements into practice. In many aspects western organizations have become less competent in managing knowledge in the last 20 years, not better in it. Our knowledge management capabilities by large are slipped. There are three key reasons for this. First, current management practice, with such concepts as lean and Six Sigma, is still very much focused on the elimination of standard tasks and processes, and management is still focused on HOW to do things, not on WHAT to do. Second, management practice is still very much directed towards operational performance measures which tend to measure quantity not quality. Third and last, partly due to the increased outsourcing trend, there is a strong tendency of treating professionals as a cost not as an asset. Despite our sorry track record in managing professionals, we are slowly but surely growing our understanding of managing knowledge professionals. This New Productivity Paradigm is becoming clearer due to interesting new initiatives and exciting research.

If we want to be able to create more productive businesses based on valuable professionals, first we need to make fundamental changes in the way we value people. We need to modify essential aspects such as leadership, value, culture and identity. Building a knowledge-sharing and knowledge-creating organization is not about telling people how to do their work. Giving your employees detailed working instructions is hardly the right move. Not only because it challenges the autonomy, pride, and professional identity of your workers, but also because knowledge processes tend to become elusive in the 21st century. Knowledge creation cannot be represented in diagrams to the same degree as an industrial or administrative process. Creativity and innovation are notoriously complex to grasp and depict in models. Process indicators are therefore at best indicative and incomplete. At worst, they distract an organization from the actual problems, shrink knowledge worker productivity, and create resistance of valuable professionals.

Some professionals are commodities, most are not

To really understand professionals and the variety within professionals, David Master's classical split-up of professionals is revealing and helps us to better understand the mystery of professional productivity.[112] David Master distinguishes four types of professionals based on the level of professional knowledge and the value customers place on the interaction with these professionals. These four types are (Figure 22):

1. **Pharmacists:** Professionals who deliver a routine service to customers with standardized processes and minimal customer interaction. For example, a bank or an IT support operator.
2. **Nurses:** Professionals with an advisory, coaching or educational role. The difference with the pharmacist is that the interaction between customer and a nurse may add significant value to the client. The bond between client and nurse is of major importance for the value of the service. Another example would be a coach, teacher or trainer.

---
112 David Maister (1997). True Professionalism: The Courage to Care about Your People, Your Clients, and Your Career, Free Press, New York.

3. **Surgeons:** Professionals who possess a high degree of expertise. Specific knowledge and creativity are essential for the value of the service provided. The interaction between client and professional is often very limited and hardly delivers any value. What matters to the client is whether the professional knows his business. Another example would be rare high tech experts such as some programmers.
4. **Psychiatrists:** Professionals who resemble surgeons in the sense that specific expertise, innovation and creativity are important, but these professionals also add a lot of value by interacting with the client. To be successful in this line of work the professional and customer will have to work together on the diagnosis of a problem and its solution. Another example would be coaches of CEO's and management consultants.

Master's model of professionalism is very revealing. First of all it shows that the importance of co-creation and therefore the value interaction varies between types of professions. In some professions interaction and soft-skills are much more important than in others. Great nurses and psychiatrists are most often talented communicators with remarkable soft-skills, while in other professions codify able and measurable skills are of the greatest importance. Secondly, it shows that standardization of services is possible in some professions. Standardization is an option when these services do not require a high level of specific tacit knowledge and where customers do not value interaction with a knowledgeable person. As is usual in the case with pharmacists. By standardizing and automating these professional services can be offered at much lower prices.

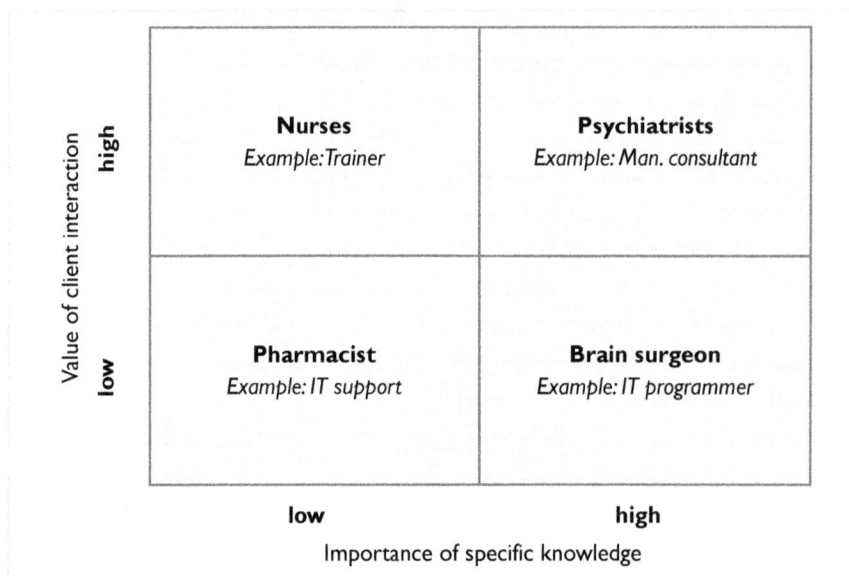

Nurses *Example: Trainer*	**Psychiatrists** *Example: Man. consultant*
Pharmacist *Example: IT support*	**Brain surgeon** *Example: IT programmer*

Value of client interaction (high / low) — Importance of specific knowledge (low / high)

Figure 22.   Different types of professionals

The model of David Maister adds to Peter Drucker's factors of production in the knowledge economy. It shows the diversity within the group of professionals and demonstrates that soft-skills are sometimes more important in value creation than hard-skills. But this model does not weaken the general importance of the factors mentioned by Drucker.

Leading professionals

As professionals have a much better understanding of their profession, the solutions and the knowledge and investment that is required for defining and implementing solutions, it is hard to judge the work of professionals for outsiders. This poses a big problem for generic managers and clients. What is the value of a certain service, what is its worth, how much does a service cost and can it be obtained in a more efficient way?

We have already established that ordering professionals, i.e. telling them how to do their work is always contra productive. This observation is essential as the share of professionals in our economy is growing exponentially. Some authors argue that the traditional role of management is over. In this view, a modern-day manager just has to make sure than s/he does not get into the way of professionals to avoid ruining their enthusiasm and natural tendency to do a good job. The knowledge professional should be facilitated rather than checked. As Henry Mintzberg said: *'A professional requires little direction and control. What they do require is protection and support.'* [113] If a manager does this, the productivity and quality will follow automatically. This view goes totally against the wonders of scientific management where hierarchy, structures, and processes are traditionally the best way to control work and workload. Similarly, the manner we reward work is still quite ancient and is based on industrial era experience. Many large corporations still use old-fashioned financial incentives to motivate their employees. We know that financial incentives work quite well in the worlds where tasks are well defined. Organizations can then use financial incentives to stimulate output levels. But the outcome of a range of studies has demonstrated that these extrinsic incentives simply do not work in environments where creativity and innovation are central to productivity. Bonuses tend to create less creative individuals who are just focused on doing their job (faster) without thinking about what they do. The focus on performance thus leads to diminishing brain power.

Managing professionals is not easy at all. Micromanaging them does not guarantee success, but giving full autonomy to them is also a wrong approach. Your clients and employees will not be happy if you give your professionals self-rule. Any managing director of a hospital or academic

---

113   Henry Mitzberg (1998). Covert Leadership: Notes on Managing Professionals, November-December.

institution can tell you that in detail. Working with professionals is actually a serious challenge. Perhaps the biggest glitch of managing professionals is that they often tend to focus on a certain domain. Obviously it is one of their strengths, but at the same time their major weakness because they often fail to see the whole picture. In most cases it is very important to mix professionals in order to get different perspectives on a certain topic. Most professionals are aware of this, but some overrate their knowledge. They have a certain point of view of a specific problem, often prescribed by a professional body of knowledge, which does not allow them to be wrong. A second and yet bigger problem is the superego professional. These are the renowned professionals who are aware that the organization for which they work is more dependent on them than the other way round. This sometimes leads to egocentric behavior. These superegos believe that the most important purpose of management and staff is to fully support them. If the organization refuses to pamper their polished self-esteem, they will threaten to leave. A third problem of a professional organization is related to the strength of informal hierarchies. Professionals enjoy comparing themselves to other professionals in their field. Professors are measured by the number of citations, doctors are evaluated by their reputation, while architects and directors are assessed by their awards. This can lead to very informal hierarchical ladders which do not foster but in fact hinder collaboration. The last problem of working with professionals is the discrepancy between the identity, norms, values, and goals of managers and those of the professionals. This gap between professionals and managers is large and difficult to overcome.

So managing professionals is tricky, but it is certainly not impossible. A well-functioning professional organization needs to ensure autonomy of professionals, provide intrinsic motivation, give people a shared identity, promote knowledge development and innovation, and give people a shared purpose. The role of the leader is thus to overcome the drawbacks of professionalism.

Connected Leadership Behaviors	Unconnected Leadership Behaviors
1. Make global connections that help them spot opportunities	1. Focus on internal connections
2. Engage diverse talent from everywhere to produce results	2. Rely on homogeneous teams for new ideas
3. Collaborate at the top to model expectations	3. Serve corporate politics and parochial agendas
4. Show a strong hand to speed decisions and ensure agility	4. Let groups get mired in conflict or attempts at consensus

Table 9.   Elements of leadership (Ibarra et al, 2011)

Overcoming these negative aspects of professionalism is not always easy. But it is clear that any management method should be based on creating motivation. In this respect, Daniel Pink argues that professionals are particularly motivated by three main essentials:[114]

1. Autonomy: professionals need to be able to determine how they work themselves;
2. Mastery: professionals have an inner urge to get better and better at something that matters;
3. Higher purpose: all individuals have a strong desire to do what we do in the service of something larger than ourselves.
4. Any professional organization which builds its leadership capabilities should base them on these building blocks of professional motivation.

Herminia Ibarra and Morten Hansen go even further in their recommendations of managing a modern professional firm. They argue that a modern leader must possess four qualities: openness, the capacity for people to connect, the ability to collaborate, and decisiveness.[115] Interesting is that the modern leader should not only be able to connect people (both inside and outside of the organization), but mostly he should be able to make intelligent choices. The modern leader must therefore have sufficient professional knowledge to assess the work of professionals and to be decisive if any disagreement between professionals emerges. Such a leader is thus not only a socially intelligent person, but is also very knowledgeable about a certain field of expertise, and, last but not least, is able to connect to a variety of different networks.

114 Daniel Pink (2009). Drive: The Surprising Truth About What Motivates Us, Riverhead
115 Hermina Ibarra & Morten Hansen (2011). Are You a Collaborative Leader?. Harvard Business. Review, July-August.

Overview

1. To add value and increase productivity in knowledge work implies that professionals and managers should focus on WHAT they should do. This requires a new type of leader.

2. Tomorrow's leaders are experts in their field and they are able to manage professionals and make tough decisions. They connect outsiders with insiders of the firm and establish a trusted yet open culture. The manager that rotates from one position to the next is something from the past.

3. Tomorrows' leaders give people autonomy, develop their mastery and provide people a higher purpose in life.

4. Tomorrows' leaders bring in an entrepreneurial culture in network of professionals to ensure that the knowledge of professionals is transformed in added value services of clients.

Part IV

MANAGING
KNOWLEDGE WORKERS

CHAPTER 12:

THE NEW HIGH PERFORMANCE SHRM SYSTEM

66 Independent workers account for 16 million people in the country now and will become a majority by 2020." Gene Zaino, CEO of MBO Partners

One of the crucial questions of the future firm is how to select the right people and skills, both in the short and long term. In this chapter we leave the topics of knowledge, networks, and leadership behind and will focus on one of the key capabilities of the modern fuzzy firm: the sourcing of professionals. Figure 23 demonstrates why sourcing is much more essential for a project based firm than a traditional firm. In a traditional firm work is a constant. Once an employee is hired, the work and function remain relatively unchanged. This is totally different in a project-based organization (PBO), because the work at hand is constantly changing due to the project modifications and new requirements. This means that the ideal person to perform the task must be able to adjust quickly to the new working situations. In other words, every project, or indeed every phase of a project, requires a new and matching professional.

The trend towards project-based work explains why staffing has become much more crucial in today's world. For every project the most suitable persons need to be found, whether they are employees of the firm, part of the organizational community or network, or indeed complete outsiders.

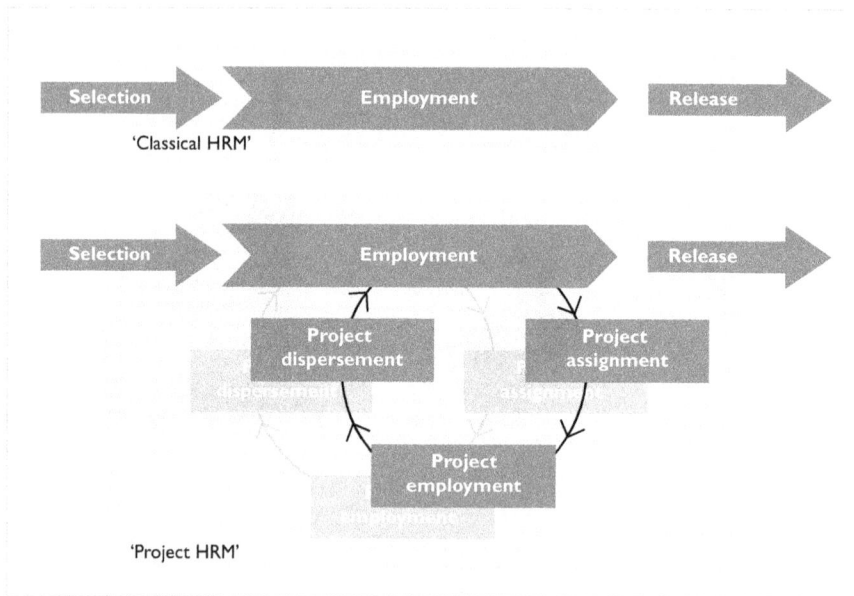

Figure 23. Constant hiring in the project based firm

The hiring decision is not a one-off decision anymore, but one of the most vital moments of truth of today's firm that largely determines the value of knowledge firm. Hiring is becoming an organizational constant and the field for hiring consultants is rapidly expanding. Not only they hire for permanent positions but also for temporary jobs for which they constantly compare internal candidates with externals.

The old model where employees stayed their entire working life with one firm is simply not always the best option in a constantly changing environment. This model restricts both individuals and organizations in their knowledge development. For organizations it implies that you have to work with generalists who miss the necessary skills to deliver successful projects and that a huge amount of effort is wasted on training and on-the-job learning. For individuals it means that they constantly have to develop themselves in new directions and cannot develop themselves in being true specialists. This may seem enjoyable, but in reality sets limits on the value of their expertise. In the long run these generalists will not be able to stand the test versus bona fide specialists.

A coherent HR strategy for attracting all resources
There are various definitions of a sourcing strategy. The exact definition really depends on the context in which the term is used. In this section we will emphasize on the networking element of sourcing. We would like to demonstrate what optimal configuration of the network would lead to fulfillment of the firm's objectives, i.e. where can we best find the knowledge that we need to create and build new knowledge and thus add value to our

clients? As we have seen such a network consist of both external suppliers (external network) and employees (internal network). The optimal network structure of a firm (i.e. centrality, density, out degree, in degree) largely depends on the kind of knowledge needed to produce new knowledge.

Currently the procurement strategy is often developed completely independently from the HR strategy (and sometimes the overall business strategy).[116] This is somewhat strange as both strategies are designed to optimally find and attract resources and capabilities to strengthen the competitive advantage of the firm. In addition, both strategies are based on the same underlying economic theories; Transaction Cost Economics (TCE) and the Resource Based View of the Firm (RBV). But, as we have already discussed, the current HR practice only focuses on attracting, developing, and retaining internal employees. It hardly pays attention to external parties. The strategic make-or-buy question is simply neither asked nor answered.

Because the strategic HR vision on external staff is often absent, there are many outstanding questions. It seems a mystery why some individuals get long-term employee contracts, and others don't. Of course, This would seem logical if internal employees and external contributors had different competences. But, more often than not, insiders and outsiders have for most part the same competences. Is this perhaps to promote internal competition and compare employees with market standards (benchmarking), or it has to do with the roles of internals and externals? Is the role of the employees to act as a mediator between different outside firms, responsible for directing and coordinating the tasks of insiders for the maximum benefit of the firm? There could also be the case of overlapping processes. A firm could use external suppliers as important channels for hiring employees. These are all relevant questions which are for the most part missing in current HR strategies. This lack of vision may lead to ineffective HR policies and an expensive HR organization which pampers low value employees, while at the same time, scarce high value professionals are treated as commodity.

A modern HR or procurement strategy must go far beyond the black-and-white distinction between internal and external employees. The distinction between internal and external professionals is contrived in many respects. The relationships between the firm and external professionals are sometimes more intense and durable than the relationships of firms with the employees. Many employees, certainly at a younger age, only remain a couple of years at a company. They are a kind of freelancers-plus, although firms invest heavily in these 'talents'. The preferences of individuals may

---

116 For a HR strategy with an explicit role for externals see: David Lepak & Scott Snell (2002). Examining the Human Resource Architecture: The Relationships Among Human Capital, Employment, and Human Resource Configurations. Journal of Management, 28, 517-545.

vary over time. Sometimes a person will opt for a long-term contract, in other times the same person may aspire a role as an external contractor. This depends on various elements such as life stage and the individual career goals. Switching between employment contracts and freelance agreements are becoming common. There is also a big increase in new hybrid forms of contracting and alternative sourcing options such as distributed work concepts such as crowdsourcing and collaboration platforms. In any case, make-buy-ally decisions are becoming an undeniable part of the HR function.

Implementing the new high performance SHRM System

Clair Brown and Greg Linden examined two different strategic HRM systems; the so-called high-commitment and the high-innovation SHRM system.[117] Currently most business in the western world use a form of a high-commitment SHRM system where organizational loyalty and identity are key goals. Only in the last 10-20 years the high-innovation SHRM system is slowly emerging, especially in the global high-technology industry where Brown and Linden did their research. In Table 9 below the key differences between the high-commitment and high-innovation system are compared.

Where high-commitment SHRM-systems typically emphasize the risks of loss of knowledge and stimulate broad skill-sets, the high-innovation SHRM-systems typically highlight the power of personal networks and the added value of specialist professionals. Some high-innovation SHRM-systems even pay for bringing in the personal network inside the community of the corporation.

Special focus in a high-innovation SHRM system goes to the management of teams; everyone should understand the vision, structure, governance and processes of the team and how it all fits together. Team building has become a key tasks in high-innovation SHRM systems. Team incentives are designed to encourage collaboration and support. Personal incentives are only used to for individual goals. Senior management is responsible for identifying talents. Those team members with extraordinary knowledge, skills, abilities and/or networks are rewarded and efforts are made to retain these talents.

The loyalty issue

There is still a lot of prejudice against working with outside contractors instead of long-term employees. One of these preconception is that outside professionals are less committed to the firm. But despite the large amount of research dedicated to the loyalty of outside professionals, much of the

---

117 Clair Brown and Greg Linden (2010). Managing Knowledge Workers in Global Value Chains, Working Paper Series, Institute for Research on Labor and Employment, UC Berkeley. http://escholarship.org/uc/item/1h3013gn

existing research shows no difference between their commitment and that of regular employees. Lucy McClurg argues that high-skilled freelancers are as committed to their sponsor organizations as 'core'-workers.[118] The project based nature of knowledge work means that freelancers quickly become part of the team and integrate into being good team members.

	High Commitment System	High Innovation System
Goals	• Long-term jobs to create required knowledge and foster commitment.	• Project-oriented hiring with state of-the-art knowledge from mobile talent pool.
Worker Mobility	• Perceived as a net loss	• Perceived as cost-effective
Job Assignment	• Chosen to develop broad skill • set, with flexible assignments • Contributions to team tasks as • well as individual task	• Chosen to exploit narrow • specialization • Work done individually or • sequentially within team
Skill Development	• Planned through formal classroom training	• Through professional networks and • project changes
Communication Flows	• Gatekeepers for external knowledge	• Individual use of external networks • Structured flows with partners • IP protection emphasized
Compensation & Promotion	• Performance-based pay to reward ongoing efforts • Small differential within cohort • Promotions based on future contribution • Steep age-earnings profile with low variance	• Bonus for project milestones with • individual rewards for specific targets • Large pay differential based on • market opportunities • Promotion of those selected to • become executives • Relatively flat experience-earnings • profile with large variance

Table 10. Comparing SHRM Systems (Brown & Linden, 2010)

In another piece of research Joanne McKeown concludes that freelancers demonstrate a much greater willingness to exert extra effort to ensure organizational success than co-workers and managers thought them capable of.[119] She argues that this willingness to exert extra effort comes from their professionalism. The identity of freelancers is very much linked with commitment to the profession rather than any individual organization. She also mentions that the time-to-contract may be an important factor in regulating organizational commitment. Freelancers who work for

---

118 Lucy McClurg (1999). Organisational Commitment in the Temporary Help Service Industry, Journal of Applied Management Studies, 31-42.
119 Joanne McKeown & Glennis Hanley (2005). Keeping contractors happy, Monash Business Review, vol 1, Monash University ePress, Melbourne Vic Australia, 44-47.

only a short time span are less likely to have significant organizational commitment than freelancers working on longer projects. It seems that organizational commitment grows over time, but in a year or so the organizational commitment of temporary professionals is not so different than the organizational commitment of long-term employees. On the positive side, research suggests that freelancers are much more committed to the success of the project than long-term employees. This should not be a surprise because the success of a project is crucial to the quality of the freelance portfolio and therefore the success of the freelancer. Not a soul wants to hire a temporary professional with a sorry track record.

Overview

1. Due to the abundance of project ornaizations, hiring becomes more frequent and more important; project hiring becomes a core competence of knowledge firms.

2. A proper knowledge organization has sourcing of knowledge at the heart of their strategy. A sourcing strategy links business strategy to both HR and procurement strategies. Only when the organization has a proper sourcing strategy, it may be able to source optimally.

3. Such a sourcing strategy is based on the type of knowledge required and produced, the maturity of knowledge resource markets and the preferences of individuals.

4. An innovative firm should implement a high-innovation SHRM system instead of a high-commitment SHRM system.

The Fuzzy Firm™

CHAPTER 13

HOW NOT TO HIRE

66 Key for any [knowledge] organization is the critical ability to move human capital skill and expertise to business opportunity – or to put more simply: to get the right person, with the right skills at the right time, place and costs."
IBM Institute for Business Value

In the past decades the world of hiring has already changed a lot (Figure 24). Twenty years ago, middle managers were not used to hire external specialists on a daily basis to help them solve specific problems. Externals were not yet part of the sourcing strategy. Almost all activities of organizations were performed in-house. But since the 1990s the share of externals in enterprises has grown slowly but surely. With this prolonged growth the perceived need for expenditure and risk control has risen. To control these apparent risks, the role and responsibility of procurement in selecting and hiring specialists have expanded since the mid-90s.In the last decade the procurement process of external staff became more and more structured using a proactive approach, tighter procedures, and much better support from IT. [120] This has made the hiring process efficient, faster, and more effective. With the involvement of procurement, the number of suppliers was also limited and often large contracts were closed with one or only a few large suppliers. These larger contracts were attractive as lower rates could be negotiated and more efficient standardized procedures could be agreed.

---

120 Nina Lindberg & Frederik Nordin (2008). From products to services and back again: Towards a new service procurement logic, Industrial Marketing Management, 37, 292-300.

Since a number of years, Managed Service Providers (MSP's) have become a phenomenon in Europe and the US. These (mostly external) providers strive to optimally support the hiring process of external staff by the optimal use and support of technology; a Vendor Management System (VMS). Such a VMS often provides the user with different functionalities such as a default catalog with fares and competences, a harmonized hiring process with workflow, automatic invoice flows, and frequent management reports on the hiring process. Different vendors can be connected to the VMS. The sponsor or client of the MSP can post vacancies and other requests for support. These vacancies, based on a number of criteria, are then sent to all vendors. Each of these vendors can then respond to these requests. The advantages of a VMS managed by an internal or external MSP seem to be considerable:

1. There is no dependence on one or only a few suppliers;
2. There is a transparent and modular process that can be customized in various ways;
3. There is an auditable process that meets the compliance requirements;
4. There are efficient hiring processes supported by state-of-the-art ICT solutions resulting in a low cost hiring capability;
5. More competition between suppliers leading to lower rates of intermediaries;
6. Rapid fulfillment of outstanding vacancies;
7. High percentage of contracts that is satisfactorily completed.

Seeing this long list of benefits it is no wonder that VMS/MSP type of solutions have become very popular in recent years. Over 80 percent of all large organizations in the United States use a VMS/MSP type of solution.

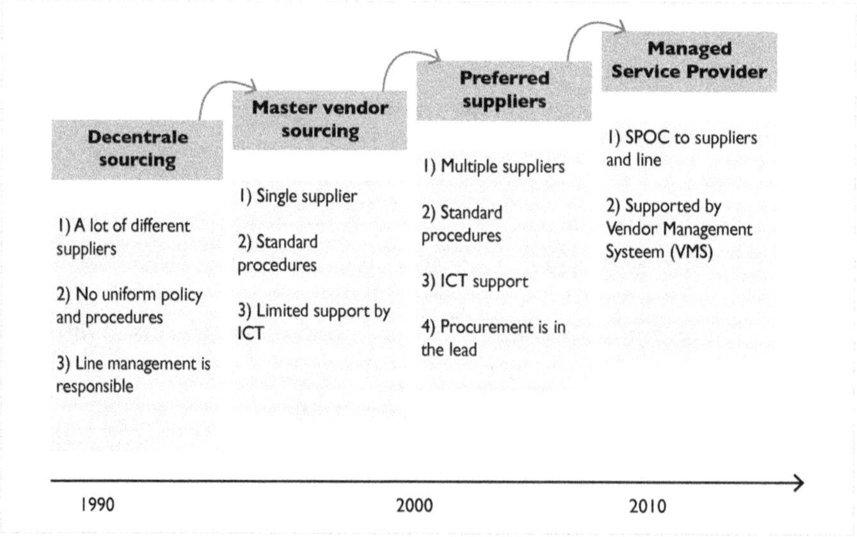

Figure 24. *Figure 24: Historic context of the hiring process*

In the United Kingdom VMS/MSP type of solutions is growing quickly. Almost half of all larger employers expect to use a VMS/MSP solution in the near future to support external staffing.

Current problems with external sourcing

With the advent of MSP's the expansion and professionalization of the hiring function has just started. Although the substantial investments in automation has resolved many problems and led to a significant decrease in the transaction costs, there are still a considerable number of persistent problems. The main problems and dilemmas are discussed below. [121]

1. With the increasing emphasis on efficiency and cost there is a tendency to treat **professionals as commodities.** But it is very hard for organizations to be innovative if they treat their employees as a commodity. [122] This is because knowledge workers will not be inclined to proactively share their knowledge with such a sponsor or employer. This will inhibit the formation of a culture of sharing knowledge that is a prerequisite for successful innovation and renewal. These allegations of Roger Byrne have been confirmed by several organizational scientists in different studies. Knowledge organizations are doomed to fail if they treat their workers as a commodity. [123]

2. With the growth of MSP's and marketplaces there is **increasing competition on price,** not on quality. But contracting against a price that is too low has multiple negative consequences:
   a. Vendors tend to offer less quality (*'if you pay peanuts, you get monkeys'*).
   b. The loyalty to the sponsor is limited and suppliers will opt for a more lucrative contract when it comes along.
   c. There is a tendency to bill more work to compensate the lower price
   The focus on cost, not on quality is strange as there is no ingrained contrast between quality and cost in knowledge services. Although it is true that specialists demand a higher fee, if these specialists are able to do the job properly in a shorter time-frame, the total cost of the specialist is still much lower than the cost of the generalist. So typically in the knowledge based services, specialists are better and cheaper. Regrettably most of today's organizations are not yet able to effectively value quality. To limit costs, they agree maximum rates for certain competencies. However this method does not lead to actual savings, but rather to low quality.

3. The **quality of many MSP's is below par.** A VMS can be managed by an MSP (more internally focused) or by an intermediary (more externally focused). In both cases it is important that the MSP understand the

121 Kim Hoque, Ian Kirkpatrick, Chris Lonsdale & Alex De Ruyter (2011). Outsourcing the procurement of agency workers: the impact of vendor management services. Work Employment Society, 25, 522-541.
122 Roger Byrne (2001). Employees: capital or commodity?. The Learning Organization, 8, 44-50.
123 Donald Hislop (2003) "Linking human resource management and knowledge management via commitment: A review and research agenda. Employee Relations, 25, 182-202.

challenges of the market and the firm. For each knowledge domain an assessment has to be made, and the MSP has to determine that availability, cost, and quality on offer on the market. This connecting feature of a successful MSP is exceptionally difficult. It requires substantive knowledge of the necessary competences and the projects at hand. The party concerned must be able to assess both hard and soft skills, and has to be the sparring partner of senior and middle management. Mostly this is not the case and the MSP is staffed with junior employees who just scroll resumes. It is very rare that these junior employees are truly trusted advisors to the management.

4. **The MSP may not be neutral.** Sometimes the MSP has a double interest; managing the service as well as supplying people. If the MSP is not neutral, it has a strong motive to present their employees or contractors. This does not always have to be a problem. In many cases this may be the most effective and efficient manner to find and select resources, but it has an inherent risk that not the best candidate is presented, but the most profitable one.

5. **One size does not fit all.** Different processes and procedures are needed for different types of competences. For some knowledge domains you need to understand the market thoroughly, while for other domains it is important that you fully appreciate the demands of the internal organization. Some competences are scarce and others are abundant in the market. For some assignments having hard skills are crucial, for others soft skills are vital. Particularly in the US more and more hybrid models are emerging where professional, scarce candidates are sourced differently than candidates for more routine work.

6. **High cost and low quality caused by too many layers.** It happens regularly that there are five to ten different layers between the professional who performs the work and the sponsor. In each layer there is another agent who tries to earn a decent penny through matchmaking. But in the end the professional is rewarded with a scanty rate or wage. In addition, contract terms are sometimes highly detrimental for the final contractor. It may come as no surprise that the delivered quality matches the low fee of the contractor and not the high fee that the sponsor is paying.

7. **Lack of socially responsible entrepreneurship.** Until know the hiring organization has not assumed full responsibility for the overall supply chain. This may lead to socially irresponsible contract terms and rates for some contractors. The hiring organization will increasingly be confronted with their responsibility in this respect. There are already high profile examples of this. Consider, for instance, manufacturers such as Nike and Apple which are held accountable for the working conditions in the factories of their suppliers

8. **No development of knowledge professionals.** Firms are increasingly looking for experts in their fields, someone who has already done the trick

several times. This is quite understandable, but this method of hiring can be damaging. For one thing, there could be too little investment done in the development of the professionals. Since professionals are only hired for doing the same trick over and over again, they will not develop their knowledge sufficiently.

9. **Tunnel vision and typecasting.** People have the natural inclination to select people who remind them of themselves and share similar experiences. This certainly has advantages such as less friction and a better mutual understanding. However, this system of attracting talent tends to lead to tunnel vision, a lack of creativity, and low performance. To prevent such a selection process, the MSP must be a trusted advisor to the management and be able to challenge management in the selection process.

10. **Selection of the wrong vendors.** A VMS allows for a much deeper market than a *single vendor or preferred supplier-like* construction. But if intermediaries are affiliated which do not possess the correct skills and networks, the potential benefits of a VMS will be offset. This would lead to higher search costs, lengthy search periods, and a low percentage of completed assignments.

11. **Flawed market insight.** By utilizing an external MSP, the organization runs the risk of developing insufficient understanding of the changes in the market and the availability of talent. Moreover, the firm understands of knowledge developments, skill levels and price/quality ratio will slowly diminish.

12. **Loss of knowledge.** Most parties do not develop long term relationships with their contractors, and the energy invested in knowledge retention is often minimal. This means that all the knowledge gained during a project is often lost to the firm and, even worse, used for the benefit of a competitor.

13. **National focus instead of global focus.** Most MSP's are still organized by country. But there is a growing need for international sourcing of available talent.

14. **Limited use of business analytics.** Currently, little use is made of business analytics. This is a missed opportunity as databases may be increasingly used to evaluate the efficiency, effectiveness, and quality of the sourcing process.

The length of the above list shows that despite the huge success of MSP/ VMS solutions, there are still important strategic, tactical, and operational advantages to be gained. More importantly, the analysis shows that customization of the MSP solution is crucial. It is certainly not a one-size-fits-all solution. The optimal sourcing strategy depends largely on the required skillset or knowledge domain. Certainly in the short term VMS solutions may lead to immediate savings, but as Kim Hoque, Ian Kirkpatrick, Chris

Lonsdale, and Alex De Ruyter show in their analysis, VMS solutions often do not lead to real savings in the long run because they tend to focus on rates and not on quality. This is certainly contrary to the principles of successful knowledge work as formulated by, for instance, Peter Drucker.

Adding a more humane elements to MSP/VMS solutions is probably the trickiest task as this goes against the core competence of the procurement department. Procurement is often pretty good in introducing procedures and controlling costs. But in the networked economy the best approach to source knowledge is quite subjective and focus should not be on controlling costs, but on attracting quality. Perhaps this can be demonstrated in the words of a senior purchasing manager: *'We're putting a lot of energy in evaluating purchasing results, but that is often very difficult. It is sometimes impossible to assess the quality of a service objectively. That is why we prefer to evaluate costs and why we have a preference for services with objectively measurable results such as business travel'*.

Current problems with internal sourcing

Above we addressed the current problems with the sourcing of external parties. The list of future challenges has proved to be quite extensive. But there are also plenty of opportunities to improve the internal sourcing process in most organizations. John Boudreau points out in his research that the current internal hiring process is typically very ineffective and inefficient.[124] There are four key areas in which the internal sourcing process should be improved significantly:

1. The various knowledge sources are not pooled. An organization has three sources or channels of human capital: 1) internal employees, 2) vacancies, and 3) external collaborators. The basic problem of sourcing is in all three cases quite identical, namely finding the right person for the job. Therefore, it might be very beneficial to look for talented individuals using all available channels at the same time and not be restricted to a certain channel.

2. There is an unjustified black-and-white view unnaturally dividing internal and external employees. The HR organization is responsible for employees. Typically the HR organization emphasizes on particular aspects such as the selection and recruitment processes, retention, employer branding, performance and remuneration systems, career paths, talent management, talent development, and working conditions. Procurement is often accountable for the external contractors. The focus here is on assignments, rates, and terms and conditions of contracts. Often the HR organization is not involved in these matters. Even in most

124 John Boudreau (2010). IBM's Global Talent Management Strategy: The Vision of the Globally Integrated Enterprise, SHRM Case Study, Society of Human Resource Management, VA.

HR strategy documents, there is hardly a line or even a single word about the role and added value of contractors. There is however a strong need for HR competences in managing these external relations. Valuable professionals require humane relations and an individual approach. HR should be more involved in recruitment, selection, retention and development of external relations.

3. In many organizations there is no clear separation between knowledge management, resource management, and project management. In these organizations there is a lack of understanding of the development, effectiveness, and efficiency of employee deployment. In some cases, this approach may lead to very effective informal organizations, but this lack of information may as well signal underutilization or underinvestment.

4. Even if organizations have information on the use and value of human resources in knowledge projects (this is often the case in professional services), this does not necessarily mean that the sourcing process is efficient and effective. In many organizations there is a big discrepancy between the available internal resources and the desired skills that are needed to deliver. This would lead to low utilization rates of resources, while important projects cannot be started at the same time due to the lack of necessary resources. This situation results in a high and mounting pressure on managers to start projects with unqualified employees. This lack of proper staffing would diminish innovation and productivity, which in return would lead to the strange situation that an influx of new projects does not contribute to profit, but instead large sums of money are spent on gig-less professionals and on unsuccessful projects.

From broker to talent agent

The core task of all intermediaries is to unite supply and demand. Unfortunately, if you are an intermediary in this day and age, your added value is probably under tremendous pressure by the advance of the internet and the advent of new business models. This does not only include the staffing intermediaries, but it also applies to a range of intermediaries in other businesses such as insurance resellers and car dealers. The added value of the traditional staffing agencies depends partly on the network that the broker adds to the organization's network and, for another part, on the additional services of the broker (e.g. selecting, recruiting, contracting, et cetera). The added value of these supplementary services depends on the skills of the professional (i.e. hard vs. soft skills, scarcity, and strategic importance). The added value of brokers is particularly under pressure at the low end of the market where knowledge is generic or certified. For these generic and certified professionals, communities, crowds, and markets are slowly replacing brokers. These marketplaces offer a much better matching function because the available set of professionals and assignments is broader, deeper, and wider. Moreover, these markets can operate at much lower costs than the traditional brokers. This can be applied to the matching of demand and supply but also to the contracting phase. However, it should be noted that searching and finding people via marketplaces is not easy. Even if the desired knowledge is quite generic or highly certified, the available supply may be too limited for markets to survive (e.g. actuaries) or the soft-skills may play a huge part in the selection process.

However, it does not mean that the role of the traditional brokers is over. It rather signals a shift from broker to talent agent. The contemporary staffing intermediary does have an important role to play in the network economy. Since the brokers have provided a good understanding of trends in the markets and developments at large organizations, they are the ideal candidates to support independent professionals with their knowledge and networks. The staffing intermediary becomes a talent agent responsible for coaching, developing, supporting, and promoting professionals. The core tasks are career development, financial support, knowledge development, and finding jobs. This level of support can be very intense, labor intensive, personal, and business aspects are increasingly interrelated.

Naturally not everyone will have a talent agent since such personal support is quite expensive. At the top end of the market, the talent agent invests in long-term relationships with scarce professionals and will actively engage in talent spotting. Talent is often spotted at a relatively young age and in an early stage of the career (or even at school). In the lower segments of the professional market, the support is much less personal, more remote, and based on far-reaching online automation of services. The name of the game is information. Platforms and databases with valuable information for specific professionals will be developed. In the next ten years we will witness increased competition between different platforms. These platforms will offer basic matching services and supplementary services using freemium business models. At this moment we do not really know how this market will develop, excepting that there will only be a few winners and many losers. Market places and crowds still have, despite a difficult start, a promising future.

The role of procurement & HR
In the previous section we argued that HR needs to be much more involved in crafting the sourcing strategy. Yet we believe that the center of gravity of sourcing should always lie in the heart of the operation (Figure 25). With ever increasing specialization, it is illogical to expect any central organization to oversee all knowledge and come up with the quality or cost assessment. The operation is ultimately responsible for the quality delivered to the customer and they have the best insight into the knowledge they need to do their job properly.

Of course it is not always easy for the managers to constantly look for talents and, at the same time, be responsible for business results. Therefore, in some cases sourcing specialists will need to support management with finding the right skills within the organization and in the market. These so-called sourcing managers are often the matching part of the project managers to staff projects. They have knowledge of a specific area and know what internal and external expertise are required and available. They are also able to challenge project managers to prevent stereotyping and tunnel vision. Because external labor is becoming increasingly important and a vital source of competitive advantage, it is logical to pay more attention to sourcing of professionals since the cost of failed and postponed projects are many times higher than the costs of setting up a proper sourcing structure.

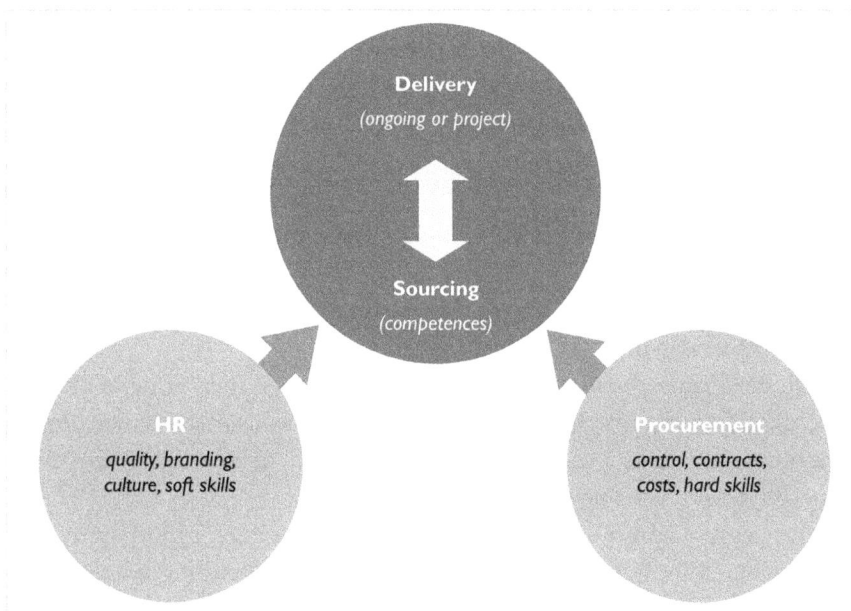

Figure 25. Cooperation between Procurement & HR

HR and procurement are important advisors of the operation in the sourcing process. Procurement has a clear focus on cost containment and control, HR has a focus on quality, organizational culture, encouraging trust, and team building. The relative importance of HR and Procurement depends on the required skill and knowledge, the preferred sourcing method, and the perceived scarcity of resources. If the firm only needs persons with generic skills, market places, contracts and crowdsourcing, the best channels may be to compile such knowledge. The role of HR will therefore be limited. The role of HR is typically much bigger if the supply of knowledge professionals with specific intangible knowledge is limited and when 'soft skills' are needed. In these cases knowledge alliances and communities need to be comanaged. The traditional skills of the HR function in the area of recruitment, selection, development, and retention are of great value in this respect. Just imagine organizing alumni meetings with individuals operating as knowledge retention guarantors and reinforcing the network of the organization.

At this moment procurement is still often the core of the operation with respect to dealings with external parties. Looking at the recent historical developments will throw light on the reasons behind the authority of procurement. Since the early 1990s outsourcing and subcontracting have been growing exponentially in almost all industries. By the end of the millennium the costs of subcontracting had become significant, but the process of procurement had hardly changed. This ensured tremendous opportunities to save costs using effective procurement strategies. This demonstrated the ability and skills of procurement. With proper restructuring of the procurement processes significant lower costs were achieved. Nevertheless, it seems that the time has come to give the HR function a bigger and stronger role in the sourcing process. There are a number of good reasons for this:

1. HR strategy and procurement strategy should be merged into a single sourcing strategy.
2. The distinction between external employees and internal employees is not black-and-white.
3. With the ageing population, the lack of resources is increasing in certain occupational groups. Since these scarce professionals may not want to be permanently employed by a single organization, firms need to use other means to establish such connections.
4. Alliances and communities are becoming increasingly important in this age of open innovation. The effort should rest in creating a culture of trust, not a culture of control.

Data analytics & the sourcing hub
A potential advantage of MSP/VMS type of solutions is that a lot of valuable information is preserved such as agreed rates, duration of assignments, success of assignments, and individual contribution to team efforts. Where the focus of these systems is largely on professional fees, this data will be increasingly enriched with information regarding the quality of vendors and individual professionals. In the future analyses of these databases will give a tremendous amount of information about the efficiency, effectiveness, and quality of the sourcing process.

It is most likely that with the emerging importance of data analytics, VMS solutions will follow the trend in the manufacturing sector where

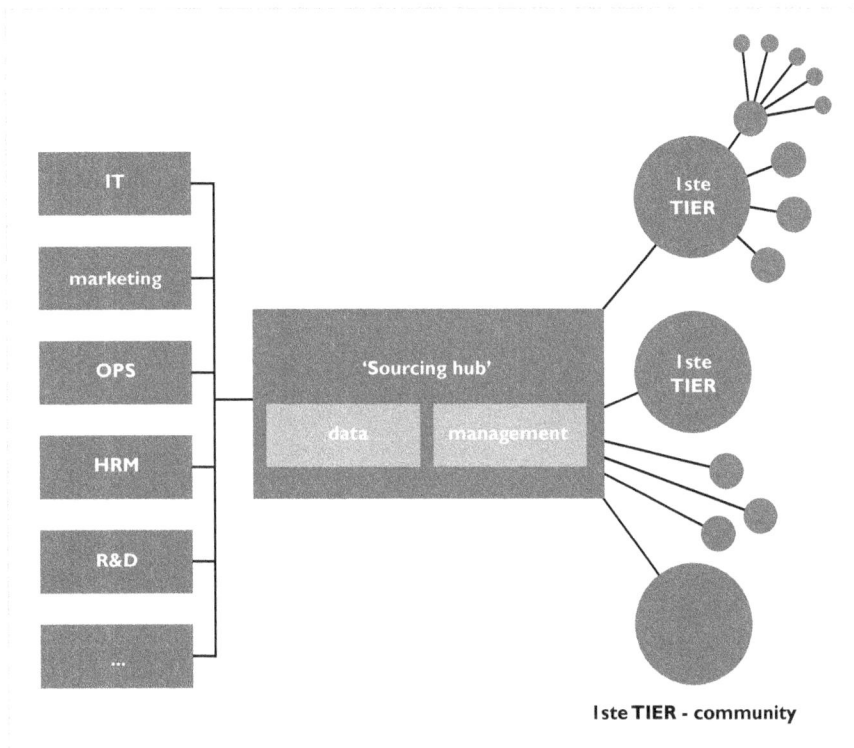

Figure 26. The Sourcing Hub

sourcing hubs are emerging.[125] (Figure 26) A sourcing hub is the source of all information (i.e. upstream data) about all suppliers, small or large. It provides insight into the costs and quality of all the sourcing relationships and it creates an overview of all the relationships of the firm. Not only of the relationships with the suppliers, but also with the suppliers of the suppliers. The sourcing hub adds value through:

1. Better investment and cooperation decisions since there is more insight in the knowledge and networks of partners.
2. Additional insight into the developments in the supply chain: where the scarce knowledge is located and how can we gain access to this knowledge.
3. Active knowledge sharing with suppliers about changes, modifications, and problems so suppliers can proactively develop solutions.
4. Source of data on all information about quality and costs of suppliers and subcontractors.

---

125 Anupam Agrawal, Luk Van Wassenhove & Arnoud De Meyer (2011). Managing Value in Supply Chain – Case Studies on the Sourcing Hub Concept. Available at SSRN.

Overview

1. The sourcing process has much improved over the last decade. Processes and systems have become much better and are much more efficient. The strengthening the role of procurement has led to a significant decrease of contractor rates and transaction costs.

2. However, there is still plenty of room for improvement in the external sourcing process.

3. There is too much emphasis on contractor rates, but almost no focus on quality.

4. Individuals are often treated as a commodity and knowledge is lost, not retained.

5. Sourcing processes and organization should put more weight on the soft side of sourcing. The focus should be on sharing knowledge, values, and identity. These softer issues are perhaps not so important in sourcing routine work, but the human side of sourcing is critical when one wants to innovate by creating and applying professional knowledge.

6. The opportunity of improvement is not limited to the external sourcing process. Perhaps the biggest achievement can be found in improving the internal sourcing process and in combining different pools of knowledge.

7. The responsibility of knowledge sourcing lies with operational management, but operational management is supported both by HR and procurement to support the execution.

8. Data analytics and sourcing hubs are basic operational tools that will see increasing use to support the management of knowledge sourcing.

PART V

WHAT'S NEXT?

CHAPTER *14:*

BACK TO THE FUTURE

In this book we have described the organization of the future. The idea of a firm will be quite different in the gig economy than it is in today's industrial and service economy. Firms have to reinvent themselves because firms will become single projects or portfolio of projects. These projects will increasingly be unique or at least incomparable to an earlier venture. These projects will be staffed with highly-skilled hyperspecialized professionals who collaborate to create something new. To achieve this, the professionals will need autonomy, a sense of purpose, and the possibility to become a master in their field of expertise. To build a career and a reputation, these professionals will hop from one challenging assignment to the next. In some cases these professionals will come across similar, capable, trusted professionals. Thus a new partnership will emerge and a boutique firm will materialize. In other instances these professionals will remain solo and become freelancers who only collaborate in projects, in communities and on platforms to find assignments and build their network and reputation. Finally, the professional may also become an employee of a larger firm. But regardless their status, whether a partner, freelancer, or employee, tomorrows workforce will always need autonomy, mastery, and a shared purpose.

Transition and resistance

In the industrialization era of the 19th and 20th century firms became progressively larger. The combination of machine and laborer replaced the traditional craftsmanship. In this century-long process, the modern corporation gradually took over the traditional position of the profession and became the core of our economic system. It shaped the identity of the individuals and, through branding, managed to differentiate and add value to products and services. As these modern corporations grew larger and larger bureaucracies emerged which needed clear chains of command. Professional managers and a professional support staff thus emerged to organize and control these large bureaucracies. With the arrival of the gig economy, this trend is reversed. Firms are becoming smaller again. The managerial staff and the support staff will slowly decline, and managers and controllers will be replaced by entrepreneurs and professionals.

	2012	**2017**
Strategy	• Market with generalists firms • Innovation is differentiator	• Specialist or linking pin? • Innovation is obligatory
Structure	• Hierarchy • Alliances	• Network management • Project structures
Systems	• Processes are supported by IT • Routine work is dominant • Place is physical • Focus on extrinsic motivation • Offices are fixed outlays • High-Commitment SHRM	• Business and IT convergence • Creative processes dominate • Place is physical and virtual with networking and collaborative tools • Focus on intrinsic motivation • Co-working 2.0 • High-Innovation SHRM
Shared values	• Shared organizational values	• Shared professional values. • Openness to others is a vital value.
Style	• Control based on process based management information	• Leader has vision and knowledge.
Staff	• Permanent employment the norm • Personal development is an individual responsibility • Managers earn more than professionals • Local sourcing	• Organization uses many sources of knowledge in addition to permanent employment. • Valuable professionals are the best rewarded • Global sourcing
Skills	• Many companies require generalists as the core-periphery model requires people to develop oneself	• Specialists in network. • Absorption and connection capacity are crucial

Table 11.   Changes in organizations (on the basis of McKinsey's 7S)

In the table above we have tried to list the main changes in the transition from traditional to fuzzy firm. It is clear that almost anything that defines a firm will change; from strategy to structure and from leadership style to staff. Even the essential roles of the firm will change. It is for this reason that we can truly speak of a paradigm shift. Nothing will stay the same.

The transformation towards a network economy will therefore not be easy and touches the very identity and raison d'etre of organizations and individuals. This implies a lot of resistance. Although there will be winners in the network economy, there will certainly be losers. This does not mean that the new economy is better or worse. The transition from an agricultural economy with its high level of craftsmanship towards the industrial economy with its high level of mechanization also led to mass resistance. For instance, in England in the early 19th century the Luddites were a social movement of craftspersons who destroyed machines. The employment opportunities of these crafts workers were rapidly replaced by a combination of machines and unskilled labor. The Luddites felt that the industrial revolution left them without work and robbed them of their professional identity. The Luddites were not alone in their protest. Karl Marx, for instance, also argued that the industrial revolution resulted in a lack of professional identity and confidence (as well as a sense of being exploited).

Some elements of resistance against the network economy can already be observed. Routine laborers, middle managements, and support staff will all see their work disappear. And just as the land lords of the 18th century, the capitalist of the 21st century will notice that the relative value of capital as a production factor diminishes. While employment of skilled professionals will only increase, professionals will be confronted with increased levels of uncertainty and global competition. Moreover, they have to learn to take on the individual responsibility for managing the career. This is not always easy and not everyone is always able to handle insecurity and take on the full responsibility. It is in these areas that we will probably witness major resistance on a macroeconomic level. This will certainly lead to major changes in labor relations and political power.

Also within organizations, there will be great resistance against transforming towards a networked organization with communities. Especially executives and senior managers will have difficulties with the transition. Most executives vividly advocate the importance of organizational loyalty (while some of them are constantly job-hopping). They often have great difficulties to accept that their most skilled and valuable professionals can walk out on them whenever they want. The fact that in the networked firm, intellectual capital is not completely owned by the firm, but owned by the professional causes even more offensive. Some CEO's and senior managers even want to force independent professionals to sign an employment contract if they work longer than a year for their organization. But why do they do this? Is it a problem if that professional prefers connecting to your firm using a flexible contract? These senior executives seem to forget that there is a big difference between loyalty towards an organization and the terms of the contract. The fact that someone's career is not fully dependent on the organizational network and the agenda of the CEO is perhaps somewhat disturbing, but it may in the end lead to much more clarity in relations and roles. Having said that, it must be acknowledged that the resistance of senior managers is not only caused by their decreasing power and control, but it lies also in their protective nature. Many of these managers only want the best for 'their' employees. They have the best intentions, but sometimes they tend to forget that 'their employees' have career, life, and opinion of their own.

The transformation towards a network organization is obviously very complicated, but if a firm really understands how to connect to professionals, for example by doing innovative and creative projects, they will certainly be able to attract the best people from the market at relatively low cost because these professionals will want to work a firm where they can develop their skills and portfolio. To deal with resistance, organizations should start experimenting. Organizations should build experience with co-creationship, communities, crowdsourcing, talent pools, social networking, and data analytics. These and other initiatives may be initiated within the context of a Work 2.0 program. This will slowly and steadily shape the internal and external sourcing function.

Strange as it may seem, the future world will not be so different from the economic structure of the dark Middle Ages. Here crafts guilds ensured the development of mastery through professional learning and quality control. The ratio between master and journeyman was limited as the economies of scale were few. But besides the required membership of a guild, professionals were members of many fraternities to build their reputation and network. Comparable professionals knitted together physically in the same street or neighborhood to distribute work and attract customers. These professionals were constantly guarding their reputation and building their image, as a strong reputation was crucial in the insecure Middle Ages and could be a life saver in difficult periods. The guilds themselves did their businesses often with large traders who bought and sold goods across many regions and countries. The guilds were certainly no monopolist as they had to compete with guilds from other cities. Once considering these issues, the parallels between the medieval world and the gig economy will become clear. Just as in the Middle Ages professionals nowadays: 1) build their reputation, 2) network, network, network, 3) value mastery, 4) collaborate extensively, 5) meet each other and develop and share knowledge on platforms (i.e. guilds and communities), and 6) compete on a global scale. There are certainly differences, but the parallel with the medieval economy is sometimes quite helpful and entertainingly.

So what?

In this book we have shared our vision of the future firm. Perhaps luckily, our fuzzy view of the future does not imply that all firms will become fuzzy. Just as it took centuries for industrial firms to surpass the traditional crafts, it will take decades before the network economy will be larger than the traditional hierarchy. Nevertheless, we believe that the competitive landscape will develop along the lines described in this book with increased collaboration between expert professionals. Despite the big picture, there may always be certain aspects or solutions that will be quite specific for a certain firm. Moreover, the greater part of this book describes the strategy and resulting processes of large organizations and it does not always apply to more humble organizations. Aspects such as sourcing hubs, VMS/MSP solutions, data analyses, and network analyses go beyond the needs of a small enterprise.

Our intention was not to question the added value of the traditional employee. In our view, firms absolutely need the long-term commitment of the core employee. The long-term contract will remain an inalienable part of the modern organization. We very much acknowledge the vision of Sumantra Ghoshal and Peter Moran who praise the employee relationships because such a long-term relationship provides the space to invest in and to learn from each other.[126] And we also agree with Janine Nahapiet and Sumantra Ghoshal who argue that the close-knit networks can support the creation of a high level of trust. Our problem is just that in practice far too many organizations resemble detention centers rather than a Bhudist center of wisdom and thought. As Manfred Kets de Vries, professor at INSEAD business school, puts it: *'Too many organizations are like gulags; extremely unpleasant places to work'.*[127] We also believe that many of today's beliefs of HPWP are essentially flawed and lead to overinvestment in generalist and underinvestment in specialists. Career paths for professionals are typically lacking and true specialism is not valued. In contrast, the only way to the top is often through ever increasing steps of management scope.

In this book we argue that the firm of the 21st century should combine the advantages of organizations (e.g. shared culture and identity) with the benefits of markets (e.g. larger pool of resources, objective information, and

---

126 Sumantra Ghoshal & Peter Moran (1996). Bad For Practice: A Critique Of The Transaction Cost Theory, Academy of Management Review, 21, 13-47.

127 Manfred F. R. Kets de Vries, Reflections on Groups and Organizations: On the Couch With Manfred Kets de Vries, INTRODUCTION, page ix.

open transparent relationships to all stakeholders). The fundamentals of such a novel, hybrid approach can be seen everywhere. Especially in the creative industry, but also in IT and professional services new and innovative forms of organization are emerging based on autonomy, mastery, and a shared purpose. New platforms, networks and communities are emerging where long-term commitment and loyalty are redefined.[128] There are great benefits of these novel forms of cooperation between professionals, for instance, more flexibility, openness, innovation, and creativity. Sure there are drawbacks of these new forms of organization. Most of these downsides are primarily felt by shareholders and management. And they simply do not have an alternative.

We show that the organization of tomorrow has progressively more methods at its disposal to attract the right resources. The long-term employment relationship is just one of these instruments. Each of these methods has specific advantages and disadvantages and is more or less suitable to bind to a particular type of knowledge to the organization. But it is certain that sourcing of professionals is quickly becoming the key success factor in many industries. At the same time it turns out to be increasingly complex. This implies that many firms will have to invest heavily in (global) sourcing. The professionalization of sourcing must start with a solid strategic assessment of knowledge requirements. Such a strategy should be supported by networks, IT, processes and, not forgetting, professionals. It is also important that organizations start experimenting with novel sourcing methods to better understand the advantages and disadvantages of different methods.

There is a **real danger** that organizations will not follow our recommendations, but instead opt for further savings in this economic crisis by:

1. **Extensive outsourcing of knowledge.** Such a strategy may seem attractive at first sight because of the huge anticipated savings, but this is actually a strategic hazard because these large knowledge outsourcing deals almost always fail miserably.[129] This is not surprising given the fact that most knowledge services simply cannot be completely outsourced.
2. **Focus on costs and not on quality.** This will prove to be *'penny-wise, pound-foolish'*. This will lead to an organization which lacks the commitment, culture, creativity, and knowledge needed to innovate and execute new ideas.

128 David Krackhardt (1999). The ties that torture: Simmelian tie analysis in organizations. In: Research in the Sociology of Organizations, Vol. 16, Andrews SB, Knoke D (eds). JAI Press: Greenwich, CT; 183–210.
129 Mary Lacity, Shaji Khan & Leslie Willcocks (2009). A review of the IT outsourcing literature: Insights for practice, The Journal of Strategic Information Systems, 18, 130-146.

What will happen if organizations do not optimize their sourcing of knowledge, but instead opt for one of the two alternatives above? Fortunately, this is easy to predict. The business case for a proper sourcing model can be written on the back of a piece of paper. Through proper sourcing projects will get under way faster and these project teams will be more successful (and more innovative). Sourcing of projects is one of the three core competences of any knowledge organization (in addition to acquisition of projects and delivery of projects). Not having a proper sourcing strategy or not being able to execute this strategy will of course have important drawback and implications for competitive advantage.

Organizations will have to strike a new balance between DYI and outsourcing. When they continue to do too much work with a limited set of generalists, they will be outmatched by specialists and their service quality will eventually diminish. In addition, they run the risk that they are insufficiently flexible to cope with new technological innovations and fluctuations in the economy. But when organizations outsource too much to suppliers simply to cut costs, mutual knowledge sharing will decrease, valuable knowledge will be lost, and innovation abilities will fade away. The strategic position of this organization will slowly but surely be eroded.

The example of the feature film industry indicates that network structures offer substantial benefits in knowledge services. It leads to more innovation, more satisfaction, a higher quality of services, and does this all at substantially lower cost than the traditional supply chain model. This sublime combination of objective productivity and subjective happiness is made possible by two factors. First, in knowledge work the value of specialists is much higher than that of generalists. Second, professionals are given full responsibility, autonomy and freedom. They are not judged on vague organizational objectives, but rewarded based on their professional results. A profession that they themselves have chosen, where their heart lies, and in which they are much better than generalists.

www.ingramcontent.com/pod-product-compliance
Lightning Source LLC
Chambersburg PA
CBHW081506200326
41518CB00015B/2393